8/19/2018

1

KISS THE SON
STEPHEN A. ADEYEMI

Kiss the Son: A Guide To A Flourishing and Intimate Covenant Relationship with God.

Copyright © 2018, Stephen A. Adeyemi

Publisher: Second Covenant Mogul Publishing LLC.

Website: www.Christiankgbookstore.co.place/wp

Cover Artist: Second Covenant Mogul Publishing LLC.

CONTENTS

ACKNOWLEDGMENTS

I want to acknowledge Jesus Christ my Lord, my Redeemer and my best Friend, The Lover of my soul and the Lifter of my head, who gave me the grace to write this book. He is the source of my inspiration, whose breath gives my writing life. Since my regeneration, He has been my Strength on every side. He instructed and directed me to write this book and He never left me in the dark as to His plan and purpose for this book. I am a product of His ineffable love and amazing grace. I cannot thank Him enough for His unfailing love and tender mercies towards me. To God be all the glory, all the honor, all powers, and adoration forever. Amen.

I also want to acknowledge and thank my parents for their unwavering support, constant encouragement, undying admonitions, and relentless prayers towards my life and ministry. You are indeed an awesome blessing to me!

I sincerely appreciate my siblings, friends, relatives, and colleagues in ministry, whose unreserved support played a role in making this book a reality. I recall with pleasure the atmosphere of love that my ministerial colleagues in the USA blessed me with.

For this and all the help I received, I say thank you to you all.

INTRODUCTION

The very core of Christianity is intimacy with God, and the laddered pages of this book will systematically guide you into this core. This book is a product of my encounters with the Almighty and a product of my relationship with the Trinity. You can't read it and not be tremendously blessed! I have always maintained that experiential Kingdom messages make the most impact, and this necessitated the inclusion of some of my immutable relational experiences with God in this book. *KISS THE SON* is borne out of divine inspiration and the practicality of divine relationship. It was written by the leading of the Holy Spirit for God's purpose for mankind to be fulfilled. I have no iota of doubt that this book will whet your spiritual appetite, stir up your desire for intimacy with God, enlighten and embolden you for the fulfilment of God's purpose, empower you to do exploits to God's glory, change your perspectives positively, transform your life for good, and prepare you for eternity with the Lord.

Tap into the eternal truths revealed therein about fostering a communicative, covenant, deeply connected, and flourishing relationship with God.

Psalm 2:10-12

"Be wise now, therefore, O ye kings, be instructed, ye judges of the earth. Serve the Lord with fear, and rejoice with trembling. *Kiss the Son*, lest He be angry, and ye perish from the way, when His wrath is kindled but a little. Blessed are all they that put their trust in Him."

Encapsulated in these three picturesque words is the deep personal intimate relationship that God covets. Second, it is a command, an imperative. We are called to kiss the Son. This cannot be done by proxy. It lays bare what the Lord wants to see flow from our hearts. These are essentially love, adoration, appreciation, relationship and of course a practical expression of our profession.

The Son in this context is Jesus Christ, our Lord, Savior and the only begotten Son of the Most High God (Luke 1:32). To kiss the Son is to get involved affectionately and passionately with Him. It is to take a dive into the ocean of His love and get immersed in His fullness. Why? He is the Author of our salvation and redemption, the most precious possession we could ever have. He alone is the pathway to God and to Heaven (John 14:6). The very essence of the redemptive work of Jesus Christ on the Cross is to reconcile us with God and restore us to a flourishing relationship with Him (John 3:16).

The one thing God loves and desires the most is a sweet and intimate relationship with men. Knowing this, the devil manipulated Adam and Eve out of God's earnest desire and succeeded in turning the sweet relationship sour. God still longs for a flourishing relationship with us, and for this sole purpose,

He sent His only begotten Son to reunite us with Him and restore us to a sweet fellowship with Him. Every blessing we attract from Heaven is by virtue of our Abrahamic covenant relationship with God. This is why we say, "Abraham's blessings are ours". We are part of that Abrahamic covenant with God as descendants of Abraham, through the redemptive sacrifice of Christ Jesus.

Mankind lost that deep and flourishing relationship with God in the Garden of Eden, but Jesus Christ the Son of God, by His strengthened passion at the Garden of Gethsemane and His death on the Cross of Calvary, gave us the greatest platform to be redeemed, reconciled, and lifted back to heights of intimacy with God. However, this wonderful redemptive and restorative platform can only thrive when you KISS THE SON.

May you be richly blessed by the Almighty Father as you read on in Jesus' Name!

PLANT A KISS ON JESUS THE SON ━━━━━━━━━━━━━

The starting point of your journey towards covenant intimacy with God is the salvation of your soul by the redemptive blood of Jesus. Jesus Christ established a covenant of redemption with us by shedding His blood on the Cross for the remission of our sins. This covenant of redemption must be engaged before covenant intimacy can be attained. To be placed on the pedestal of covenant blessings with God, you must believe in Jesus Christ, acknowledge and accept Jesus as your Lord and Savior, confess your sins, ask the Lord for mercy and cleansing by the blood of Jesus, forsake your sins, and you must declare an unending love for Him and an undying commitment and consecration to serving Him.

It is essential to establish that planting of a KISS on JESUS is the only way to attract divine blessings, divine attention, command divine intervention, contact divine illumination and access divine information. All these and more are ultimately born out of a cordial relationship with the Son – Jesus Christ, our Lord, and Redeemer. Thus, we would consider the word "KISS" as an acronym which stipulates the ways to get into an intimate and flourishing covenant relationship with God. Beloved, to have a great relationship with God, you must indeed **KISS**.

Kiss The Son

A Guide To A Flourishing and Intimate Covenant Relationship with God.

CHAPTER 1

K- KEEP HIS LAWS

The laws of the Lord are to be kept if His face is to be seen and His blessings are to be received. Every relationship is premised upon principles. A relationship without principles cannot thrive, and it would eventually become an object of ridicule. Principles regulate and revitalize relationships, and this truth comes to play in establishing a great relationship with God. Passion, compassion, and affection are only empowered to thrive on guiding principles. Keeping the Laws of the Lord is a key principle in establishing a covenant relationship with Him. It cannot be overemphasized! "But he that keepeth the law, happy is he"- Proverbs 29:18b.

No one can experience an intimate and flourishing relationship with God without keeping the Laws of God. To keep the Laws of God is to concentrate on the Laws, to cling and commit to the Laws, to carry out the Laws of God, and to constantly and completely obey his Laws. No one gets close to the Lord without making the most of His Laws. The Laws of the Lord are His precepts, commandments, admonitions, and dictates as expressly revealed in His Word. Simply put, the Laws of the Lord are the Words of the Lord. Every Word of God becomes a law the moment it is revealed for our profiting. While communicating with Joshua, the Lord described His Words as the Book of the Law.

"This Book of the Law shall not depart out of thy mouth..." Joshua 1:8a

Joshua, the son of Nun, was a mighty man whose life and ministry was characterized by uncommon exploits due to his amiable and enviable relationship with God. By him the sun stood still, the wall of Jericho fell and the children of Israel experienced the wonders and glory of victory. But these great and amazing feats achieved by Joshua were made possible by virtue of his obedience to keeping the Laws of the Lord. Joshua obeyed God's commandments completely, followed His leading strictly, and carried out His instructions constantly without compromise. Like Joshua exemplified, these are prerequisites for establishing and maintaining a free-flowing covenant relationship with God.

The Lord God speaking to Joshua said:

"Only be thou strong and very courageous, that thou mayest observe to do according to all the law, which Moses my servant commanded thee: turn not from the right hand or to the left, that thou mayest prosper withersoever thou goest" Joshua 1:7.

God gave Joshua a clear and precise instruction and admonition which he strictly adhered to, and which ultimately became the platform for his elevation. You can't get it wrong with God when you keep His Laws and you can't sink with the world if you keep His Word. The Laws of the Lord are the Words of His covenant. God is a Covenant Keeper! Jesus Christ established a new covenant with us by His death on the Cross. As indicated earlier, He established the covenant of redemption and reconciliation. The Lord said in His Word, "My covenant will I not break, nor alter the thing that is gone out of my lips" – Psalm 89:34. God is absolutely faithful to His Words; He is not a covenant breaker. When you are a law keeper, God would manifest Himself to you as a Covenant Keeper. When you keep the Laws of the Lord, He would fulfill His covenant promises for your life as embedded in His Word. The Lord delights in your obedience to His Words. Nothing moves God to act on behalf of a man like obedience. Obedience to the Laws of the Lord provokes divine intervention, deepens and cements your relationship with God, and it serves as a catalyst for Kingdom glory, Kingdom greatness, and joy. Without obedience to God, you cannot overcome the trials of life, the fiery darts of the wicked and the forces of darkness. Obedience to God puts you in command of dominion, deliverance and destiny decoration. Obedience to the commandments of God is the foundation of a flourishing relationship with Him. The Lord rejoices over the obedient and He showers His blessings upon them. The Lord will not rejoice over anyone who rejects His Laws, and the rejoicing of God over you is the catalyst for a rich relationship with Him. Don't reject the Laws of the Lord, but rather receive them and live by them in absolute surrender.

"And Samuel said, Hath the Lord as great delight in burnt offerings and sacrifices, as in obeying the voice of the Lord? Behold, to obey is better than sacrifice, and to hearken than the fat of rams." 1 Samuel 15:30

The best way to please God is to obey His Words. When you dedicate and consecrate yourself to keeping the laws of the

Lord, the Lord Himself would make you a Kingdom heir, kingdom relative, and an affiliate.

Thus, the explosion of your kingdom relationship with God!

Obedience to the voice of the Lord is the pathway to victory. Obedience to the instructions of God is the gateway to elevation and unending celebration. Abraham became a friend of God because he walked according to the laws of God. We should emulate what is good and eschew evil after the order of Abraham, the only man ever to have a direct covenant with God, an enviable relationship, a covenant that can never be broken and whose descendants we are as believers through Christ Jesus. A relationship with the Lord cannot be established if your adherence to His laws is not ascertained. The eyes of the Lord do not behold iniquity, and He cannot have a romantic relationship with the abominable.

Kingdom Romance is real because God is love and His greatest desire is to have an intimate relationship with us. Don't abdicate the place of Kingdom romance, appreciate it! Get into a romantic relationship with the Lord now by kissing the Son. The Lord is craving for an intimate relationship with you, and to come to the actualization of this, He is saying to you, "Keep my Laws".

"So when they had dined, Jesus saith to Simon Peter, Simon, son of Jonas, lovest thou me more than these? He saith unto Him, Yea, Lord thou; thou knowest that I love thee. He saith unto him, Feed my lambs." John 21:15

After making Peter the pillar of the New Testament Church, Jesus the Son of God asked him a question and gave him an instruction simultaneously. It is noteworthy that for the purpose of affirmation, Jesus the Son repeated this question and instruction three times.

From the above, we can depict that our response to divine questions and instructions matters so much to the Lord. As he doles out the instructions, He demands an instantaneous response from us. We can see interpersonal communication being engaged between our Lord and Peter; and Peter's immediate response to the words of our Lord Jesus. This is a model of a flourishing relationship. Delayed response or delayed obedience to the Words of the Law would alter and negatively affect the flow of our relationship with Him. In order to sustain a flourishing relationship with God, you must Obey the Lord promptly, instantly, immediately, and completely! Communication is the bedrock of every relationship, and effective communication is characterized by feedbacks. Jesus the Son got an instant feedback from His question to Peter, and because the feedback was satisfactory and sufficient, He also gave a corresponding instruction, which Peter obeyed unreservedly after the ascension of the Son of God. The Bible recorded the many gospel exploits of Peter which was activated on the platform of his relationship with the Son of God- Jesus Christ. Having received the gift of the Holy Spirit through the cordiality of his relationship with Jesus Christ the Son of God, Peter preached boldly in the company of other Apostles and five thousand souls were added to the church in one day. More so, the shadow of Peter healed the sick, the lame walked, and many signs and wonders were made manifest through Peter, because of the sufficiency of divine power that has been made available to him through his thriving relationship with the Lord. Beloved, an intimate relationship with God would launch you into realms of the miraculous and wondrous. However, your zeal for keeping the laws of the Lord must be evergreen, with no signs of respite and converted into practical and evidential works of obedience.

Contrive to engage in an intimate relationship with God by keeping His Laws at all times and at all costs. God our Creator never does anything without a purpose, and He created us for the sole purpose of having an intimate relationship with Him. He exemplified the core purpose of our creation by frequently communicating with Adam and Eve. Alas, Adam and Eve fell to the deceit of the devil by breaking the law of the Lord, thereby, leading to the break in the relationship between God and man. By this, we can cogently establish that the moment you break the laws of the Lord, you break your relationship with the Lord. The moment you disagree with, despise, deny, or disapprove the laws of God, you activate a disconnection with God. The worst thing that can ever happen to a man is to be disconnected from God. This is because when a man is disconnected from God, his life is opened up for the devil to operate in and tamper with. May your life never become an operation ground for the devil and for works of darkness in Jesus' Name. May the Almighty God bestow upon you the grace to remain connected to Him in Jesus' Name.

Whenever you keep the laws of the Lord, you have Kissed Him, but whenever you break the laws of the Lord you have kissed the devil. We know this because the Lord said to Prophet Elijah in 1Kings 19:18, "Yet I will leave 7,000 in Israel, all the knees that have not bowed to Baal and every mouth that has not kissed him." Baal was a devilish Idol which had its prophets, and the Lord also had His prophets, which included Elijah and 7,000 people in Israel. In the light of this, we can affirm that those who KISS the Son are preserved by God, but those who kiss the devil will never enjoy the grace and covenant blessings of God. According to Proverbs 24:26, the Lord kisses the lips of anyone who gives the right response to His covenant demands. Therefore, KISS the Lord by keeping His words, so that you may draw Him close to you to kiss you.

Keeping the laws of the Lord is central to the establishment of a flourishing and intimate covenant relationship with Him. Therefore, keep His Laws delightfully, and you will experience His benevolence ceaselessly.

Kiss The Son

A Guide To A Flourishing and Intimate Covenant Relationship with God

CHAPTER 2

I - INTERACT WITH HIM

The ability to interact with the Son through His Holy Spirit helps you to successfully navigate through inevitably stormy situations in life. Interaction with the Son gives you access to divine information and divine information is what you need to be rightly placed in the pursuit of life's purpose, peace, glory, joy, and prosperity. Divine information saves you from impending shame and from looming evil plots. I've been privileged by grace to be privy to divine information about forthcoming temptations, about agents of darkness and evil agendas, about my rapture-status, and about my destiny.

Many times, the Lord would audibly give me corresponding prayer points to terminate the bad and triumph in the good. It is a blessed and richly-satisfying thing to have access to divine secrets. The Bible says, "The secrets of the Lord is with them that fear Him and He will show them His covenant" – Psalm 24:14. God reveals His secrets to those who diligently serve Him and interact with Him. If you want to blossom and prosper, then you need divine information which connotes visions and revelations. Just dedicate yourself to the Lord and cultivate the habit of interacting with Him through the Kingdom interactive means that you would learn as you progress in the reading of this book.

Like Joseph, divine information through dreams from God would enable your drive, determination, and focus in your journey to fulfilling destiny. Understand that your spiritual elevation is dependent on divine information. God uses His voice, His dreams, His visions, His revelations, His written Word, His angelic visitations, His inspiration, and His prophets as conduits for divine information. The catch is that as you build up your spiritual sensitivity by engaging the guides revealed in this book, God would reveal Himself in an amazing way to you.

Only God knows the way through the wilderness and only God knows the future. Therefore, it is wise to seek His face by interacting with Him, in order to know the right way to go and the right steps to take in the journey of destiny.

Ideas for inventions and innovations are made manifest on the platform of divine information. Men who don't interact with God for access to divine information would miss God's plan for their destiny and God's purpose for their lives. Catastrophic marriages are prevalent in our societies today because humans have refused to seek the face of God for direction. Many are wallowing in the sea of ignorance and have found themselves in spiritual hot-water just because they do not purposefully interact with their Maker for divine information. I pray that by virtue of divine information, the Lord will deliver you from the wicked and cruel kingdom of fruitlessness in the Name of Jesus.

Expect to hear from God every day. Expectation precedes manifestation. God honors our expectations as long as they are in accordance with His will and in alignment with His purpose for our lives. Expect to get divine Information on a daily basis. It is possible! The Scripture records in Proverbs 23:18 that your expectations will not be cut off. I crave earnestly to hear from God every day of my life. This is because I know that my ability to reach my glorious destination hinges on divine information. Before 24 hours is over in a day, always make sure by all spiritual means, that you hear at least one word from God. The word of God is power, and it empowers you in the pursuit of purpose and for the fulfillment of destiny. Devote time every day to seeking the face of God and to reaching the heart of God for divine information. The voice of God empowers! When you hear from God you are empowered to scale heights of honor, glory, victory, greatness, joy, fulfillment, favor, wisdom, power, dominion, courage, and prosperity. Therefore, covet to hear from God and consecrate yourself to Him, so that He'll be committed to speaking to you and directing you always. It pays to interact dedicatedly with God.

Divine information which came through Interaction with the Son was what ushered Simon Peter into his abundance. We can see the account of Peter's interactive encounter with the Son in Luke 5:4-6, "And when He had left speaking, He said unto Simon, Launch out into the deep, and let down your nets for a drought. And Simon answering said unto Him, Master we have toiled all the night, and have taken nothing: nevertheless, at thy word, I will let down the net. And when they had done this, they inclosed a great multitude of fishes: and their net broke." We can infer from this account that Simon Peter interacted with the Lord, used the information given to him by the Lord, stemming from their interaction and the Lord terminated his toiling, struggling, fruitlessness, and failures. It was on the platform of interaction with the Son that Simon Peter got the information which culminated in his transformation and celebration.

More so, his transformation via this productive interaction with the Lord skyrocketed him into fulfilling a higher purpose. Simon the fisherman became Peter the fisher of men! After he – Peter accepted the kingdom message from the Son and responded favorably to Him, he was given a Kingdom mandate, which made him one of the foremost disciples of Jesus Christ and a great pillar in Christianity. Just by engaging interactively with the Lord, Peter got massively blessed and gracefully placed. A lot of blessings accrue unto us through divine information which comes from our interaction with the Lord.

It is imperative for you to know that interaction with the Lord begets His intervention. Your voice is a tool of victory as long as it is engaged with and for the Lord. God values your voice! Your voice is an instrument through which God is served the meal of pleasure. He wants you to use your voice constantly to interact with Him. This gets Him delighted, as it emphasizes our dependence on Him and dedication to Him. Our Lord loves those who commune with Him and He concentrates on them. He is absolutely committed to those who commune with Him. "Should I hide my plan from Abraham?" the Lord asked"- Genesis 18:17. What a divine privilege it is for Abraham to get firsthand information about the moves of God upon the earth. You should desire that because the information you get via your interactive relationship with God informs your decision, and your decision informs your direction, and your direction informs your destination.

The Bible recorded that Abraham was a friend of God, who had a knitted conversational relationship with God. "And so it happened just as the Scriptures say: 'Abraham believed God, and God counted him as righteous because of his faith.' He was even called the friend of God"- James 2:23. What a great privilege it is to be called the friend of God. You should crave to become a friend of God and not just a child of God. Constant interaction with the Lord moves you from sonship into friendship with Him. The Lord can be your best friend if you always interact with Him. The Bible says, "The Lord is a Friend to those who fear Him. He teaches them His covenant"- Psalm 24:14. Abraham, the patriarch of faith was a man who had an intimate and flourishing covenant relationship with God. We can affirm this by what the Lord said to Abraham in Genesis 17: 7, "I will confirm my covenant with you and your descendants after you, from generation to generation. This is the everlasting covenant: I will always be your God and the God of your descendants after you." Considering this, we as covenant children of God and of the covenant lineage of Abraham should walk in the way Abraham walked and tread the path that he trod if we want to become friends of God and experience the unending benefits of having a covenant relationship with Him. In following Abraham's relational steps, you become obedient to the Lord's core will, which is to have an intimate and flourishing relationship with you.

God created you to relate with you, but you can't have an intimate relationship with God if you don't interact with Him. Intimacy thrives on the scale of interaction. Do you know that God can allow you access into His privacy if you are in an interactive relationship with Him? Yes, He can! I once had a very rare divine privilege, where God opened my spiritual eyes in the middle of the night to see four saints in Heaven. God said to me in the spiritual realm, "Look up," and when I looked up to the sky, I saw a great lightning pierce through the clouds into the firmament which split Heaven open. Then I saw Elijah, Moses, Peter, and Paul embracing each other, rejoicing, and radiating the glory of God. In fact, I saw Moses beckon on Elijah to come close to him and they embraced each other joyfully, with Peter and Paul coming into the frame. They were together in a very beautiful and shinning room in Heaven, they wore very fine and colorful garments and they smiled so beautifully. As I saw these Heavenly scenes, I was overjoyed and full of motivation to make Heaven by all means and against all odds, in order to join these saints in this blessed and glorious rejoicing.

For the first time, beyond the joy of my salvation, I experienced joy unspeakable full of glory. After this sweet experience, my zeal for the Lord fired up, my faith in Him increased, I became even more unflinching in my propagation of the gospel and I became unflappable with renewed sobriety in rendering my service in the Lord's Vineyard.

Beloved, it is on the basis of your intimacy that the Lord would allow you access into His privacy and get divine secrets that will help you blossom upon the earth and shine brightly even into eternal life. Opportunities and platforms for prosperity are always around you, just ask God to open your eyes to them. By virtue of my graceful interactive relationship with God, I once heard the voice of the Lord saying to me, "I will give you platforms to prosper, but avoid dullness." Shortly after this time, opportunities for prosperity were opened to me, and I am still diligently engaging those opportunities for my lifting while ensuring that any form of dullness is not tolerated in my life. Beloved, God is committed to leading you to your promise land if you interact dedicatedly with Him. The Lord knows the way through the wilderness, just commune with Him and He'll carry you through. The Lord literally invested in my spiritual life by allowing me by divine privilege into His privacy – letting me see Heavenly places, visions of rapture, angels singing and so on, this empowered me to be more obedient to the Heavenly vision and it prompted me to self-examination and to the watchfulness of obeying God without reservation.

It is paramount for the Christian life that you engage daily in interacting with your Maker, thereby, causing His grace, glory, goodness, and secrets to ceaselessly flow towards you. The Lord would invest greatly in your life if you interact with Him frequently. Therefore, make it a point of duty to interact with God on a daily basis.

You are probably very familiar with the story of Abraham interacting with God to rescue the righteous from perishing in the sinful lands of Sodom and Gomorrah, but let's draw some insights from it. You will discover some treasures from this story which would transform your life for good. When God told Abraham of His plan to destroy Sodom and Gomorrah due to the wickedness and rebellion of those cities, Abraham asked God to spare the people because his nephew Lot lived in Sodom. In fact, Abraham engaged in a lengthy conversation with God to mediate for these cities. His interaction with God led to a timely and profitable negotiation. Understand that you are always presented with an opportunity for a righteous negotiation with God on the platform of your interaction with the Lord.

We shouldn't miss such opportunities to establish a glorious purpose. You can make a covenant with God over any issue of your life during your interaction with Him; and because God is a covenant Keeper, He would faithfully fulfill His own part for your joy while you faithfully fulfill yours. God honors His covenant! Concerning His covenant, the Lord said in Psalm 89:34, "No, I will not break my covenant; I will not take back a single word I said." The Lord's absolute commitment to keeping His covenant was affirmed in this passage of Scripture and you must constantly lay it to heart that when you make a covenant with God during your interactive sessions with Him, He would be utterly committed to keeping the covenant for your glorious purpose to be achieved.

Hannah wanted a male child after being barren for many years, and she interacted with God in the place of prayers and engaged a covenant negotiation with God through a vow. "Hannah was in deep anguish, crying bitterly as she prayed to the Lord. And she made this vow: 'O Lord of Heaven's armies, if you will look upon my sorrow and answer my prayer and give me a son, then I will give him back to you. He will be yours for his entire lifetime and as a sign that he has been dedicated to the Lord, his hair will never be cut."- 1Samuel 1:10-11. After this interactive activity, the Lord answered Hannah and gave her a son- Samuel; Samuel became the foremost prophet of Israel and did exploits for the

Lord. Beloved, nothing moves God to a speedy action than a covenant made with Him. When you make a covenant with God, you activate the integrity of God over that situation or circumstance, you attract the attention of the Lord over that issue, you enjoy the blessedness of a covenant relationship with Him, and you experience the manifestation of your expectations.

I enjoin you to interactively enter into a covenant with God over your life and destiny and see how God would jealously guard you, guide you, supply your needs and quicken the manifestation of your expectations. Covenant negotiations, on the basis of covenant interaction, strengthen our covenant relationship with God.

Abraham's relationship with God is one that all Christians should covet and learn from. He engaged the power of interaction with the Lord to get the promise of intercession. You should covet this, and run with this understanding in order to have an intimate relationship with God. What you don't covet, you can't contact or command. Proverbs 10:24b says, "What the righteous desire will be granted." Therefore, if you don't desire an intimate covenant relationship with God, you don't deserve it. What you desire is what you deserve! You should covet and desire an interactive relationship with the Lord, which would place you on a flourishing and intimate pedestal with Him. Abraham wanted God to spare the righteous people who lived in Sodom and Gomorrah, so he negotiated with God on their behalf. He asked God, "Will You sweep away both the righteous and the wicked? Suppose You find fifty righteous people living there in the city- will You still sweep it away and not spare it for their own sakes? Surely You wouldn't do such a thing, destroying the righteous along with the wicked. Why would You be treating the righteous and the wicked exactly the same! Surely You wouldn't do that! Should not the Judge of the earth do what is right? And the Lord replied, 'If I find fifty righteous people in Sodom, I will spare the entire city for their sake.

Then Abraham spoke again, "since I have begun, let me speak further to my Lord, even though I am but dust and ashes"- Genesis 18: 23-27. He pressed further in his conversation with God in the subsequent verses and God did spare Lot and his two daughters as a result of Abraham's interaction with Him. Abraham wanted to see his own extended family protected from God's judgment and prevented from destruction. Hence, he engaged in an interaction with God to negotiate their exemption from judgment and destruction. God did spare Lot – Abraham's Nephew and his two daughters as a result of Abraham's interaction with Him.

This largely shows that you can become an instrument of redemption through your interaction with God. There's no limit to the glorious heights you can attain if you constantly interact with God.

Commune with God as a friend with Friend. Make known your desires, expectations, cravings, delights, appreciations, and acknowledgments to Him. He loves this absolutely. He feels the Joy as your Heavenly Father indeed when you interact with Him, just as you'll feel overwhelmed with joy when your little baby calls you "dad" or "mom". Our Creator wants to have a great relationship with us and that relationship is made possible on the platform of interaction.

When you commune with God regularly, you become immune to evil attacks and to every work of the devil. Our God is an interactive God, and He makes His intentions towards us known through our interaction with Him. Cultivate the attitude of interacting or communing with Him and great will be your rewards.

You can interact with Him through 3 Keyways:

- **Through His Spirit** – The Spirit of the Lord is the Holy Spirit. The Holy Spirit is the spiritual channel through which we can interact or communicate with the Lord. The Holy Spirit has been mandated to communicate the Lord's intentions, plans, and purposes to us and get our responses to these messages and convey them to God. "When the Spirit of truth comes, He will guide you into all truth. He will not speak on His own but will tell you what He has heard. He will tell you about the future"- John 16:13. The Holy Spirit speaks the mind of God to us, the Holy Spirits relates the agenda of God with us and expresses God's desire towards us. The Holy Spirit interacts with us, guides us, leads us, strengthens us, and inspires us. You can hear the Holy Spirit audibly, you can feel and hear the Spirit speak to your heart, you can feel the impression of an idea or a direction in your mind and you can see Him through the written Word of God.

Intimacy with the Lord cannot be achieved without an interactive relationship with His Spirit. I've had some amazing interactive experiences with the Holy Spirit. As I share some of them with you, I want you to lay it to heart, that the Holy Spirit Speaks in every language- audibly and inaudibly, and the Holy Spirit sings – with awesome melody, great, simple, insightful lyrics, amazing rhythm, heavenly sounds and sweet spiritual tunes.

The first time I heard the Lord speak audibly to me through His Spirit was a couple of years ago, at around 3.am, on a Church' campground in Africa. While sleeping, laying on a long wooden chair, after the program, then suddenly I felt a divine presence by my side and I heard a still and tender Voice saying to me 3 times, "The Big Wow! The Big Wow! The Big Wow!" The Lord by His Spirit spoke audibly to me for the first time and these words transformed my life, renewed my zeal for the Lord and empowered me to do great exploits for the Kingdom. After hearing these heavenly words, I woke up with a wonderful smile on my face, full of joy, I repeated those words, "The Big Wow!", and I responded to the Lord, saying, "God the Holy Spirit, thank you for calling me the big wow, what do you really mean by calling me the big wow?" Immediately, the Holy Spirit responded to me, not audibly this time, but by speaking to my heart, interpreting and explaining those words to me. He made me understand that Heaven is rejoicing over me and that I've become a wonder even to God and God would make me a wonder amongst men. He said that I've won with

God and I will experience the Wonders of Winning, which is actually the Acronym for WOW. I still give deepest appreciation and praise to the Lord for this encounter.

On another divine occasion, the Lord visited me in my room, while I was lying on my bed half-asleep at midnight, and He spoke audibly to me through His Spirit, saying, "Do you know how much I love you?" I heard Him so clearly as if He was right on the bed beside me and this blessed romantic question got me overwhelmed with joy.

The Spirit of God reiterated and reaffirmed God's love for me, but I was pleasantly surprised that God could ask me such a blessed question – "Do you know how much I love you?" I could feel the presence of the Lord in my room, so I jumped out of my bed and responded to His question by saying, "Lord, thank You for loving me so much. Your love for me is deeper than the depths of the seas and wider than the oceans." Upon responding -to the Lord's passionate question, I heard a light laugh. O yes, I heard the sound of the Lord's light laughter.

Apparently, He smiled at my response and He made me hear His light gentle laugh. In fact, I knew it wasn't a loud laugh but a gentle calming laugh that felt so refreshing and this made me really glad. From the above encounters, it is evident that an interaction took place between me and the Spirit of God. This came to be because, since my regeneration, I've consciously and wholeheartedly walked with the Lord. This encounter manifested because of the relationship I have with the Lord through righteousness and it further strengthened my friendship with the Lord and engendered our intimacy.

Since then, I've experienced and enjoyed even greater interactive encounters with the Lord through His Holy Spirit.

I've had different interactive encounters with the Lord but for the justification of this book, I've decided to share some. As you read on, you would find more relational encounters that I've experienced in the course of my graceful journey with the Lord.

I enjoin you to dive into the reality and practicality of these testimonies to activate your intimacy with the Lord which hinges on your interaction with His Spirit.

- **Through Prayers** – Praying to the Lord is a divine privilege that has been given to us to activate the purpose and promise of God for our lives. Praying is the process of communing with God, communicating your desires, intentions, and expectations to the Father. Whenever you pray with passion as our Lord exemplified in the Garden of Gethsemane, pouring your heart to the Lord in holiness and without distraction, God would respond to you somehow, someway.

Until you see the process of prayer as an interactive one, you'll never get the full rewards of prayer. It is very crucial to pray with understanding. When a righteous man prays to the Lord, the Lord responds promptly.

Though His response may come in different ways, the spiritual sensitivity of the man would enable him to hear or see the response of the Lord. Praying to God is equivalent to interacting with God.

It is a time where you express your concerns, your cravings, and your longings to the Lord. Have this understanding now, that whenever you are praying to God, you are interacting with Him. Hence, you should expect to get a response from Him. Develop the appetite for praying to God in the Spirit. Our prayer antenna must be efficient in order to connect with divine frequency - where favor is attracted and power is gained. One of the keys to connecting to divine frequency is praying in tongues.

By virtue of the Holy Spirit of God in us, we have been empowered to pray in tongues mysteriously so that we would be launched wonderfully and gloriously into great heights in spirit with the Lord. I urge you to pray in tongues daily, for it works wonders.

Jesus the Son of God gave us a model of prayer when asked by His disciples to teach them how to pray. Let us consider this prayer model revealed by our Lord Jesus in Matthew 6:9-13. Jesus said, "After this manner, therefore, pray ye: Our Father which art in Heaven, hallowed be thy Name. Thy Kingdom come, Thy will be done in earth, as it is in Heaven. Give us this day our daily bread. And forgive us our debts, as we forgive our debtors. And lead us not into temptation, but deliver us from evil: For thine is the Kingdom, and the power and the glory forever. Amen."

This prayer model is a communicative and interactive one. It depicts the possibility of a conversational relationship with God, which engenders intimacy with Him. It is characterized by Worship –"Our Father which art in Heaven, hallowed be thy Name", Absolute Surrender – "Thy will be done in earth, as it is in Heaven", Requests – "Give us this day our daily bread. And forgive us our debts, as we forgive our debtors. And lead us not into temptation, but deliver us from evil", Praise – "For thine is the Kingdom and the power, and the glory forever", and Faith – "Amen".

In the light of this, we can unmistakably say that prayer is an avenue through which our Worship, Absolute surrender, Requests, Praise, and Faith is made known to God.

Therefore, your prayer must always accommodate these 5 components in order to get divine acceptance which ultimately culminates in divine visitation and divine contact. Whenever you pray to the Lord, engaging these components in righteousness, the Lord would respond favorably to you, and His responses often come promptly. However, be spiritually sensitive and spiritually attentive to grab God's response after you've reflected these 5 components while communicating with Him. I encourage you to cultivate the spiritual habit of interacting with the Lord frequently through prayers if you want to have a flourishing and intimate relationship with Him.

Here's one of my spiritual experience with the Lord in the place of prayers. A few years ago in my living room, around 1.am, I went on my knees and started praying fervently to God, asking Him for the multiplication of His mercy upon my life, so that I may experience miracles in every sphere of my life. I was desperate for miracles so much in my life at that time and I knew that without the mercy of God being provoked and multiplied upon my life, I wouldn't have access to His miracles. After praying for about an hour, I felt the presence of the Lord in my living room and the ground began to vibrate. At first, I trembled, but I was emboldened by the Holy Spirit. By virtue of this unusual happening, I knew that the Lord was around me, so I kept my eyes closed and began to pray even more for His miracle-provoking mercy. A few minutes later, I felt an unexplainable peace in my heart, which gave me the assurance that the Lord has answered my prayers. I rounded off with thanksgiving, and I stood clapping to celebrate the Lord for visiting me and for confirming that my prayers have been answered and requests granted. The most shocking part of this experience is that as I was at the verge of leaving the living room for my bedroom to go back to sleep, the Lord spoke to me, saying "Stop! Look!" Then I stopped consciously and looked unconsciously towards the table in my living room where I left my Bible. Amazingly, I saw my Bible opened and I began to shiver because I knew that my Bible was closed before I started praying. Apparently, and without an iota of doubt, I knew that the Lord had opened my Bible. Pleasantly wowed, I quickly reached for my Bible to read the chapters and verses that the Lord had opened for me.

To my utter amazement, everything I saw and read was reflecting my answers. The Lord opened my Bible to the book of Psalm, and I saw and read Psalm 47:17-20, Psalm 50, Psalm 51, Psalm 52, Psalm 53, Psalm 54, Psalm 55, Psalm 56, and Psalm 57:1. The Lord heard my prayers and responded with these Bible passages, which had 3 central themes - mercy, trusting in the Lord, and answers to prayers.

This experience of mine goes to prove that God responds to our prayers, thus, making prayer a form of interaction with Him. If the Lord could respond to my prayers in this form, He would respond to your prayers whenever you pray. We have been admonished by the Word of God that we should maintain the attitude of praying. 1 Thessalonians 5:17 says, "Never stop praying."

- **Through Praise** – Another interactive way to have an intimate relationship with the Lord is Praise. Whenever you praise God in truth and with all your heart, He's prompted to respond to your situation. Praise is interactive; hence, it calls for a response. Praise prompts God to action. Whenever you engage in the praise of the Lord, the Lord swings into action to turn your situations into testimonies. Praise the beauty of the Lord's holiness, praise His majesty and supremacy, praise Him for His creations, praise Him for His wonders, and praise Him for His greatness. Praise Him in tongues. Sing songs of praise with spiritual and mysterious languages. Praise Him with musical instruments which include your voice and your hands. Sing, clap, and dance to the Lord of Hosts. Psalm 149:3 says, "Let them praise His Name in the dance: let them sing praises unto Him with the timbrel and harp." Psalm 47:1-7 also affirms the imperativeness and indispensability of praise. "O clap your hands, all ye people; shout unto God with the voice of triumph. For the Lord most high is terrible; He is a great King over all the earth. He shall subdue the people under us, and the nations under our feet. He shall choose our inheritance for us, the excellency of Jacob whom He loved. Selah. God is gone up with a shout, the Lord with the sound of a trumpet. Sing praises to God, sing praises: sing praises unto our King, sing praises. For God is the King of all the earth: sing ye praises with understanding." The King of kings and Lord of lords desire our most holy praise! Compose lyrics, melodies, and rhythms in your heart to the praise of the Lord your God. Joshua 6:20 reveals that the shout of praise upon God's instruction, brought down the wall of Jericho. "When the people heard the sound of the rams' horns, they shouted as loud as they could. Suddenly, the walls of Jericho collapsed and the Israelites charged straight into the town and captured it." Physical and spiritual barriers and barricades can be pulled down through praise. The integrity of God can be speedily provoked through praise. Praise God with a new song! Compose songs for your Lord and the Lover of your soul and eulogize Him always. Praise Him with Hymns. Jesus loves Hymns! Our Lord and His disciples sang hymns together while He was on earth. Matthew 26:30 says, "And when they had sung a hymn, they went out into the Mount of Olives." Hymns and spiritual songs are one of the necessities of Christianity. Hymns provoke solemnity and sobriety, which helps us to establish and maintain an intimate relationship with God. For the purpose of this book, I strongly recommend these Hymnal Songs to you: Close to Thee – by Fanny J. Crosby, Nearer my God to Thee – by Sarah Flower Adams, Draw me nearer – by Fanny J. Crosby, and Deeper, Deeper in the Love of Jesus – by Charles P. Jones. I urge you to interact passionately with the Lord through these hymns as you seek to be established in a covenant intimate relationship with Him.

Praise is one sure way to quickly get to the heart of God and attract the intervention of God over your situation. The more you interact with God through praise, the more He intervenes in your affairs, thereby leading to more intimacy. Praise opens the way to the Throne of grace and it creates a bond between you and God. Whenever you eulogize God, tell of His goodness and greatness and testify to His glory, you provoke Him to get closer to you and draw you closer to Himself. The Lord's faithfulness to you is sure, but it is activated even more on the platform of praise. Psalm 22:3 shows us that our Lord is holy and enthroned on our praises. Since our praises put the Lord on the throne of our hearts, imagine what glorious things we could accomplish by engaging praise.

I have had great divine encounters and divine interventions through praise, and I can tell you assuredly that praise works wonders! In 2015, I was praising God with all my heart and with dancing and singing in my living room, when suddenly, I felt an inner prompting by the Spirit that something unusual was about to happen. Immediately, I lifted up my eyes, and I saw the shadow of Angel's wing. The Angel was dancing and praising God with me – moving his wings to the rhythm of my praise songs. It was like a movie before me. I was in awe. At a point, I stopped dancing and began to watch the movement of the Angel's wing until he disappeared. It was an awesome privilege given to me by the Lord, to have His Angel dancing and praising Him with me. Prior to this time, I had always called on the angels of God to dance to the Lord with me, lift up their hands in praise with me, sing to the Lord with me; and I always believe that the angels do heed my calls. But on this occasion, the Lord opened my eyes to see His angel dancing and praising God with me. I saw the right wing of the angel reflecting through the light in my living room, and the sight was wonderful. It is still fresh in my memory even as I write this book. I want you to draw strength from my experience and engage in the praise of the Lord like never before. Just the same way I attracted divine presence by praise, you will always attract divine presence whenever you praise the Lord wholeheartedly. "Let the godly sing for joy to the Lord; it is fitting for the pure to praise Him" Psalm 33:1. The Lord demands our praise and He delights in it. The more you praise God, the more the Lord is informed about your intention to bond with Him. Praise brings down the glory of God! Thus, to attract His glory, you must sing His praise. Ensure you interact with the Lord through praise, for praise is the way to the heart of the Lord and it is an instrument for divine intervention and for intimacy with divinity. Enormous blessings would accrue to you if you continually praise God and continually ascribe all glory to Him. When you praise God diligently, He would bless you richly. God rewards those who diligently praise Him and He responds to their needs. David said in Psalm 34:1,"I will praise the Lord at all times. I will constantly speak His praises." This shows us that speaking the praises of the Lord to the Lord's hearing is the gateway to ceaseless blessings from the Lord and a flourishing relationship with Him. No wonder, the Lord referred to David as the man after His own heart. No wonder David learned and understood the mystery of Kissing the Son with praise in order to get the best of God the Father and become intimate with Him. Interact with the Son through Praise!

Kiss The Son

A Guide To A Flourishing and Intimate Covenant Relationship with God

CHAPTER 3

S- STUDY HIS WORD

Engaging in the study of the Word of the Lord cannot be overemphasized in the place of intimacy with Him. This is because the Son is the Word Himself and the Word is God Himself. Thus, studying the Word of the Son is studying God Himself and until you know God you can't get the best of Him. The knowledge of the Word empowers you to be in command of the world. Jesus the Son is the Word, and the Word is God. We find this Kingdom truth in John 1:1-3:

In the beginning, the Word already existed. The Word was with God, and the Word was God. He existed at the beginning with God. God created everything through Him and nothing was created except through Him.

Studying the Word of the Lord is a sure way of knowing the Lord, getting close to Him and becoming intimate with Him. Every Kingdom privilege is accessible to us by knowledge of the Word. Jesus Christ the Son is the eternal Word and the gateway to eternal life. Embracing and studying His Word places us on a gracious and glorious path with Him, which ultimately yields into intimacy with Him. Paul the Apostle in his second letter to Timothy, by the leading of the Holy Spirit said, "Study to shew thyself approved unto God"- 2Timothy 2:15a. This is an admonition that must be strictly adhered to by us children of

God if we are to enjoy the blessedness of intimacy with God. What does it mean to be approved unto God? It is to be accepted, acknowledged, and appreciated by God. It is to be adopted by God and affirmed by God. It is a great thing to be approved of God. But this divine approval for intimacy cannot be accomplished without having delight in studying the Word of God. "Oh, the joys of those who do not follow the advice of the wicked or stand around with sinners, or join in with mockers. But they delight in the law of the Lord, meditating on it day and night" – Psalm 1:1-2. Whenever you study the Word of God or meditate upon it, you trigger the mind of God towards you. If you rightly divide the word of God constantly, you'll be able to rightly discern situations, messages, and circumstances, no wind of false and adulterated doctrines would toss you here and there.

I've gotten so many revelations from studying the Word of God which has led to my transformation. Those who ruminate on the Word, get illuminated by the Word. Psalm 119:130 reveals that the entrance of God's Word gives light and understanding to the simple. This passage of Scripture reflects the importance of the Word in the life of men. The Words of God that penetrates your soul in the process of studying would be the compass through which you'll successfully navigate in this world to your glorious destination, and it'll open your spiritual eyes to see God and understand God. Great exploits would be the order of the day for those who know God and who are intimate with Him. Daniel 11:32b reveals that they that know their God shall be strong and they shall do exploits. The knowledge of God which empowers men for exploits cannot be gained without studying His Word.

You cannot do exploits for God without understanding God and have a treasure trove of God's Word in you.

The Rhema that you get through studying and meditating on God's Word empowers you to be a winner and conqueror on earth and a winner in your race to Heaven. The Rhema is the revelatory message behind the written Word and the insight behind the inscribed Words. It engenders spiritual maturity and helps in the maintenance of spiritual sanctity and integrity. Any Spirit-filled believer who constantly studies the Word of God and meditates on it will overflow in Rhema. The source of the Word of God is God, and anything that has God as its source would experience an endless flow of covenantal virtues from God. Once the source is God, the flow is endless. Begin to study God's Word on a daily basis, so that you will experience the endless flow of Rhema and Biblical virtues that will make you a Kingdom wonder. The Holy Bible was inspired by the Holy Spirit and written by vessels of God for our profiting. Let's make the most of it by devoting ample time daily to study and meditate on it.

If you don't have the knowledge of God through His Word, you cannot become intimate with God; and until you become intimate with God, you may continue to struggle. Challenge yourself to study chapters or verses of Scripture every day. Joshua 1: 8 says, "Study this Book of Instruction continually. Meditate on it day and night so you will be sure to obey everything written in it. Only then will you prosper and succeed in all you do."

Prosperity, success, and intimacy with the Lord are inevitable if you're committed to studying and meditating on His Word. People who downplay the significance of studying the Word of God, cannot have access to the Throne of Grace, and cannot thrive in the Lord. Ignorance of the Word of God has led many into the ditch of life and into perpetual failure. You have the Bible at your disposal. The Word of God is available to you. Grab it, study it, meditate upon it, and memorize it. Don't underestimate memorization of the Word. Memorization of the Word develops, delivers, and distinguishes a Christian. Memorization of Scriptures and its application will lead to the actualization of destiny. The Power of the living Word of God was established to make you a living proof. Don't let the power of the Word pass you by. Grab that power by dedicating yourself to studying the Word of God day and night. Cultivate that attitude of studying the Word of God that you may establish a great relationship with Him.

Kiss The Son

A Guide To A Flourishing and Intimate Covenant Relationship with God

CHAPTER 4

S- SACRIFICE FOR HIM

Having an intimate relationship with God cannot come without Sacrifice. The Christian life is a life of Sacrifice. The lifestyle of unending sacrifice launches you into an eternally sacred relationship with the Lord. Everyone that ever had an enviable covenant relationship with God, had it on the platform of sacrifice.

The Living Sanctuary

The Word of God establishes that your body is a living sanctuary, which should be sanctified in order to accommodate the Spirit of God and to enable an intimate relationship with God. Apostle Paul admonished the Corinthian Church saying, "Know ye not that ye are the temple of God, and that the Spirit of God dwelleth in you. - 1Corinthians 3:16." Furthermore, he said, "And what agreement hath the temple of God with idols? For ye are the temple of the living God; as God hath said, I will dwell in them and walk in them; and I will be their God and they shall be my people - 2Corinthians 6:16." These admonitions by Apostle Paul encompasses the attributes and the very essence of our relationship with God. It stipulates the necessity of holiness and total separation from the works of the flesh in order to attract a divine relationship. It also reveals that there cannot be a relationship with divinity without purity in the body. You must ensure that your body is and remains undefiled in order to establish a free-flowing relationship with God. A defiled man can never meet the Lord's demands. A defiled man cannot have access to the things of the Spirit. A defiled man cannot come boldly to the Throne of Grace. A defiled man cannot fulfill God's purpose for his life and God's plan for his destiny. A man that is defiled is automatically set up for defeat. Refuse to be defiled! In Daniel 1:8, we find the account of Daniel, who purposed in his heart that he would not defile or pollute himself with the portion of the food and drink of an idolatrous king. Daniel was determined not to defile himself, no matter how sumptuous the meal was and how hungry he was. This should always be our resolve in the face of trials and temptations. Like Daniel, we must constantly engage discipline to resist defilement. We must be willing and ready to sacrificially accommodate any form of inconvenience in order to attract divine acknowledgment and divine acceptance. Every refusal to any form of defilement comes with a tangible sacrifice. This is because the pleasure of sin is often sweet, but the end is always very bitter. The eyes of God cannot behold iniquity, hence the need to stay away from every form of defilement. Sin separates us from God and associates us with the devil. 1John 3:8a reveals that anyone who commits sin is of the devil. Sin detaches us from God and attaches us to the devil. Cling on to the old rugged cross and to the faith of our fathers. Don't blend with the unholy trend! Don't blend in with the patterns and programs of the world, stand out for God. Be the light of the world, be the salt of the earth, and dare to be different! Any man walking in sin cannot walk with the Lord. If you want God to draw near to you and walk with you, avidly avoid sin. Therefore, it is essential for you to genuinely repent of your sins and surrender your all to Jesus Christ the Lord. Repentance is of necessity because, once your character is depraved, you will be deprived of a blessed relationship with the Lord. You just cannot afford to miss the blessedness of intimacy with the Lord. In Psalm 66:18, we find the words, "If I regard iniquity in my heart, the Lord will not hear me." This buttresses the importance of righteousness and the implication of sin in relation to our relationship with God. Iniquity in the heart incapacitates us to walk with the Lord as Abraham and Enoch walked, but righteousness in the heart would position us to receive the remarkable from the Lord and to relate intimately with the Lord. Note that walking with God connotes an intimate relationship with God. But a man without the Spirit of God cannot walk with God, hence, the need for the indwelling of the Holy Spirit which places us in Heavenly heights - to relate freely, flourishingly and boldly with the Lord. Pray fervently for the baptism of the Holy Spirit, "For all who are led by the Spirit of God are children of God – Romans 8:14." The Spirit of God cannot dwell in an unholy place, and you cannot establish holiness in a place without sacrifice. The Lord once said to me very clearly and audibly, "defending Holiness is wisdom." This eternally-true words of the Lord imply that living a holy life and standing up for holiness makes you wise. So what is the wisdom in Holiness? Psalm 24:3-6 gives us the definitive answer. It says, "Who may climb the mountain of the Lord? Who may stand in His holy place? Only those whose hands and hearts are pure, who do not worship idols and never tell lies. They will receive the Lord's blessing and have a right relationship with God their Savior. Such people may seek You and worship in Your presence, O God of Jacob." This passage is a pointer to the truth that without holiness, you cannot have a relationship with God, you cannot attract the presence of God, and you cannot enjoy the covenant blessings of God. It is therefore wise to be holy because it brings forth tremendous covenant benefits. Holiness attracts God to you and when God is attracted to you, He associates with you and ultimately elevates you to glorious heights. The sacrifice of holiness is the most worthwhile sacrifice in springing up an intimate relationship with God - which is the best accomplishment a man can ever have. The lifestyle of holiness which the Lord has called us unto is the lifestyle of sacrifice. Holiness involves sacrificing the pleasures of the world for treasures in Heaven. God's Word says, "think about the things of Heaven, not the things of earth"- Colossians 3:2. Holiness involves sacrificing the pleasures of sin for the pleasures of righteousness. Think about this! You will find out that the pleasures of righteousness far outweigh the pleasures of sin. The pleasures of sin are temporal and lead to sorrow, damnation, and destruction, while the pleasures of righteousness are everlasting and lead to joy unspeakable full of glory, glorification in Heaven and eternal life with the Lord. It is wise for you to choose the pleasures of righteousness, for therein is your relationship with God and great blessings from the Lord. Psalm 16:11b says, "At Thy right hand there are pleasures for evermore." The right hand of God is full of righteousness. The everlasting pleasures from the right hand of God's righteousness become the portion of anyone who sacrificially lives in holiness to please the Lord. Give the Lord your loyal devotion and your unending sacrifice of holiness.

Without pleasing the Lord sacrificially in all things, we cannot attract the peace of the Lord that surpasses human understanding. Our relationship with the Lord, which is established by pleasing the Lord, has been ordained by God to bring his Peace upon our lives. Jesus Christ the Son of the living God is the custodian of peace; He is the Prince of Peace. So whenever you please God sacrificially, He rains His peace upon you. The Christian life is a sacrificial life! Our Master, Lord, and King – Jesus Christ gave His life sacrificially for the remission of our sins and for our redemption from the world of sin and death. He painstakingly bore our guilt and carried our sorrows. He gave His life for us on the Cross of Calvary. He died for us. What are we giving Him in return? How are we reciprocating His great love for us? All He demands from us is that in Holiness, we sacrificially make ourselves living sanctuaries, acceptable to the living God. God wants you to sacrifice your totality if you want to have an intimate relationship with the divine. Give the Lord your all in absolute surrender and resolute sacrifice. But never forget that what makes a sanctuary acceptable and habitable to the Lord is the sacrifice of holiness that is put in place.

"And so, dear brothers and sisters, I plead with you to give your bodies to God because of all He has done for you. Let them be a living and holy sacrifice – the kind He will find acceptable. This is the way to worship Him. Do not copy the behavior and customs of this world, but let God transform you into a new person by changing the way you think. Then you will know God's will for you, which is good and pleasing and perfect"- Romans 12:1-2.

Brethren, if your commitment to God is questionable, then your service to God is not reasonable. What makes your service reasonable in the Lord's Vineyard is the heartfelt commitment that is shown with attendant sacrifices. Therefore, endeavor to sacrificially render a reasonable service to the Lord, and He would cause you to flourish in Him. When you sacrifice yourself to God in holiness, you would partake in the inheritance of the sanctified. Simon Peter's statement in Acts 20:32 affirms this: "And now brethren, I commend you to God and to the word of His grace, which is powerful to build you up and to give you an inheritance among all those who are sanctified."

Simon Peter, who became an ardent soul-winner, partook in the inheritance of the sanctified by becoming the foremost pillar of the gospel of Christ after he had sacrificed his ship for Jesus Christ. Note that Jesus Christ first bid him sacrifice his ship before he - Peter could have a relationship with Him. Luke 5:3 says, "And He entered into one of the ships, which was Simon's, and prayed him that He would thrust out a little from the land. And He sat down, and taught the people out of the ship." The sacrifice of Simon Peter brought him into a sacred relationship with the Son of God. He gave his ship to the Lord, and in return, secured an enviable relationship with the Lord. This shows us that sacrifice is imperative to establishing intimacy with the Lord. Had Peter refused to give Jesus Christ his ship, he would have been lost, forgotten, and destroyed perpetually. He would have been replaced, he wouldn't be remembered from generation to generation and he wouldn't have reached the

Kingdom of God. Peter's sacrifice brought Jesus closer to him and this led to an intimate relationship with Jesus. The Lord desires your sacrifice of giving, your sacrifice of praise, your sacrifice of thanksgiving, even your sacrifice of soul-winning. Your sacrifice will bring the Lord closer to you. Covenant relationships are established on the platform of covenant sacrifices. If you want your relationship with God to continue, you must be willing to sacrifice continually for Him. Endeavor to sacrificially engage in a continuous relationship with the Lord till His Kingdom comes. The rewards and blessings for so doing are enormous and tremendous and they extend into eternal life with the Lord.

Be a living sanctuary that will constantly sacrifice your all to please the Lord in order to have and maintain an intimate relationship with Him. If you want to be satisfied in Jesus, you must be willing to sacrifice for Him.

GIVE UP YOUR 'SHIP'.

Having seen the result of Peter's sacrifice in the establishment of his intimate relationship with the Lord, it is important for us to deliberate on the 'SHIP' that we must sacrificially give up in order to gain a covenant relationship with God.

Sequel to our inferences from Luke 5:3, where Simon Peter gave the Lord His ship to be used for the glory of the gospel, we would be considering the word – SHIP as an acronym representing the things we should sacrifice for the manifestation of a sacred and intimate relationship with the Lord. You should sacrifice:

S – Self and Success: Sacrificing one's self to gain intimacy with the Lord is worthwhile. Giving yourself to the service of the Lord is an honorable thing. Until self is crucified, God cannot be glorified! Until you immerse yourself into the perfect will of God, you cannot emerge as a Kingdom star. You attract divine connection and divine commendation whenever you give up self and secular successes for the sake of the gospel. To sacrificially engage your energy, your time, and secular successes for the enlargement and propagation of the gospel is to invite the Lord to walk with you. If you are committed by sacrifice to the things of God, He will be committed by covenant to bless you indeed and enlarge your coast. To give up self is to lose self-will to the will of the Lord. To give up successes is to use successes for the glory of God and to use successes as a platform for the gospel to thrive. God gave you the life that you have and He desires that you use it for his glorious purpose.

The Lord said, "If you try to hang on to your life, you will lose it. But if you give up your life for my sake, you will save it"- Matthew 16:25. Here the Lord was simply admonishing us to give up or sacrifice our personal ambition for God's vision for our lives. He is calling our attention to reject self-will and accept God's will. More so, the Lord highlighted the danger of not being in tandem with His purpose for our lives. The Lord said it expressly without mincing words, that whosoever would continue to hold onto his life, and not give it up as a living sacrifice to God, shall lose it. Give your life to the Lord and let it be consecrated to Him. May you never lose that blessed life that God has given you in Jesus' Name. Let's take a cue from the life and ministry of Apostle Paul. Paul exemplified a life of great sacrifice for the course of the gospel, and he did great exploits for the Lord. He gave up his Jewish name Saul and took up his Roman name Paul, for the sake of the gospel. Paul means "little" or "small". Thus, he aspired to portray himself as small and present Christ as great. He was a legal practitioner, but he gave up his legal profession in order to be in alignment with the Heavenly vision. While speaking to King Agrippa, Paul affirmatively said, "I was not disobedient unto the Heavenly vision"- Act 26:19. This affirmation should be our stance if we desire a blessed connection with the Lord.

Give up fleshly lusts and allow the Spirit of God to dominate you. Give up the works of the flesh, which is characterized by immoral, sinful, and abominable acts. A carnal man cannot be connected with God. You must give up carnality if you want a relationship with the Trinity. Only a spiritually-minded man could be spiritually sensitive to receive from God. No carnal man can associate with God, for God is pure and cannot stand the sight of evil. Give up every form of carnality now. Nail them on the cross of Calvary and embrace spirituality, which puts you on a relational pedestal with the Almighty. More so, a life of carnality would ultimately lead to calamity. A life without Christ is shattered dreams. A life that is still harboring the sinful nature of satan cannot attract the presence of God. If you refuse to do away with the nature of sin, the Lord would stay away from you. In the light of this, I enjoin you to penitently give up sinful nature, embrace holiness and righteousness and engage spirituality in order to enjoy the daily benefits of a covenant relationship with God.

Willingly Sacrifice Self and Successes

You should be willing to sacrifice your earthly ambition for the Heavenly vision. God expects us to be willing and obedient with respect to His vision, agenda, plan, and purpose for our lives. God would immensely reward your willingness to obey Him sacrificially. In Isaiah 1:18, the Lord expressed His commitment to rewarding your willingness to give up self and to rewarding your obedience to the heavenly vision. He said, "If ye be willing and obedient, ye shall eat the good of the land." You just can't get it wrong with God. He is your Maker! Be willing to give up anything and everything to please Him. Be deliberate in your daily walk with God. Like Apostle Paul, be willing to give up your totality for a glorious relationship with the Trinity. In the year 2017, God spoke audibly to me, saying, "It is the willingness in your obedience that I reward." As I pondered on these divine words, the Holy Spirit prompted me to book of Isaiah chapter 1 and verse 18, which we earlier inferred from and I drew great strength from this passage of Scripture to further enhance my relationship with the Lord. I understood then that a sacrifice from a willing heart is what is acceptable to the Lord and is thus rewardable. I enjoin you to willingly sacrifice yourself and your successes to the Lord, for with this comes great rewards.

H – Household and Honor: The Lord expects us to sacrifice our household and our earthly honor for His own glory. Many times, we try to hold back members of our household from giving a reasonable sacrificial service to the Lord- be it our wives, husbands, children or our relatives. The Lord is calling us to give up our family and prestige. Abraham's enviable covenant relationship with God was established because he gave his heart and his household wholly to God. He was even willing to sacrifice his only son Isaac just to please the Lord. Translating Abraham's sacrificial actions into today's world, some of us find it really hard to dedicate our children to the Lord and train them in the way of the Lord. We sometimes give them a seeming right of way to disregard and dishonor God. As revealed in Genesis chapter 18 and verse 18, we children of God have been positioned to share in the covenant blessings of Abraham. But the question is, are we willing to pay the price of sacrifice like Abraham? Are we willing to tread the path of sacrifice that he trod? If we want to walk with the Lord as Abraham walked, we must give up our household and our honor for the Lord's glory after the order of Abraham. The Lord affirmed Abraham's commitment to giving up his household for His glory by saying, "For I know him, that he will command his children and his household after him and they shall keep the way of the Lord, to do justice and judgment; that the Lord may bring upon Abraham that which He hath spoken of him. – Genesis 18:19. The utmost desire of God is that we give up our desires for His.

Furthermore, Jesus Christ sacrificed His honor to die for us, thereby redeeming us from sin and reconciling us with the Father. Jesus sacrificially and in submission to the will of God the Father, gave up His glorious Throne of Honor in Heaven to take up the form of man. While sacrificing His honor, He was humiliated for our sake. He was beaten, spat upon, bruised, battered, despised and rejected for our sake. What a sacrifice of honor! The Son of God sacrificially accepted this humiliation so that we would not be rejected by God. He suffered humiliation for our honor. The Word of God reveals the huge sacrifice that our Lord engaged in our redemption, regeneration, justification, and glorification. Isaiah 53:4-5 says, "Surely He hath borne our griefs and carried our sorrows: yet we did esteem Him stricken, smitten of God and afflicted. But He was wounded for our transgressions; He was bruised for our iniquities; the chastisement of our peace was upon Him and with His stripes, we are healed."

Jesus Christ, our perfect example, lived a life of sacrifice on earth, in absolute submission to the will of God and for the reflection of the glory of God. Jesus Christ the Son of God sacrificed His honor to re-establish and rekindle our relationship with God; hence, as worthy disciples of Him, we should be like Him. We should be engrossed in the readiness to sacrifice our honor for the glory of God and for an intimate relationship with God. Prophet Isaiah said, "Then I heard the Lord asking, "Whom should I send as a messenger to this people? Who will go for us?" I said, "Here I am! Send me" – Isaiah 6:8. Isaiah's sacrificial resolve should be our watchword – "Here I am! Send me." Isaiah sacrificially obliged to become a messenger. Being a messenger literally is not an honorable thing. But accepting to become one for the honor of the Lord is rewarding. Giving up your honor to become a messenger comes by the deliberate and conscious exertion of sacrifice, not by coincidence. Your heart must accept it before your acts would reflect it. I urge you to engraft the word of God in your heart and enact His admonitions of sacrifice for the establishment of a blossoming relationship with Him.

I – Intellect and Inventions: The Lord expects us to routinely and demonstratively give up our intellect and inventions for His own use. The Lord is the giver of your talents and gifts, so He desires that you use them for His glory. As we have seen, God is not a user, He is a rewarder and He adequately rewards sacrifice. Every act of sacrifice to the glory of God comes with attendant rewards. The admonition and affirmation below is a proof that God rewards sacrificial labor.

Therefore, my beloved brethren, be ye steadfast, unmovable, always abounding in the work of the Lord, forasmuch as ye know that your labor is not in vain in the Lord. – 1Corinthians 15:58.

Whenever you labor sacrificially for the Lord using your intellect and inventions, you get ample rewards, which would also culminate in a blessed relationship with God. Give your intellectual resources to the Lord. Use your intellectual prowess to the glory of the Lord. Sacrifice your intellect and inventions for the use of God. Have you invented anything? Are you a manufacturer? If yes, I enjoin you to sacrificially use your inventions and innovations for the service of the Lord. Use your smartness, intelligence, and creativity for the propagation of the gospel. Give your intellect for the enlargement of the gospel. Sacrifice your talent for the triumph of the gospel!

Your song to the Lord should be, "take my intellect and use, every power that thou shall choose." Let this become your reality and God would ensure that your relationship with Him is upheld. Give up your best for the Master!

P – Possessions and Positions: The humility of a man is what gives him the ability to sacrifice or give up his possessions and positions for the course of the gospel. A high-minded man cannot be heavenly minded. A man who is chiefly concerned about his titles cannot be deeply connected to the divine mantle. God would not go all the way for you if you are not willing to go all the way for Him. As much as the Lord desires an intimate relationship with you, He demands worthwhile sacrifices from you. What have you given up sacrificially for the glory of God? What have you done painstakingly for the propagation and expansion of the gospel of Christ? I beseech you to engage in what I call "radical sacrifice" or "desperate sacrifice". This kind of sacrifice prompts God into a wonderful covenant relationship with you. It is a sacrifice done out of desperation for an encounter with divinity and for a covenant relationship with the Trinity. It is a sacrifice borne out of desperation for a connection with God. I was in my dad's car one day, in Parkville, Maryland, USA, when the Lord spoke to me clearly about desperate obedience. The Lord said, "Obey my words desperately." Before this time, I've never associated obedience to God with desperation. I had always maintained that we should obey God without reservation. But that day, the Lord alerted me to a mysterious panacea for laxity and negligence in the place of obedience to His words: "Obey my words desperately." Upon assimilating and pondering on these words with the Holy Spirit, I discovered with scriptural backing, that absolute obedience to God always comes with resolute sacrifices. No man truly obeys God without giving up something. Abraham is a typical example of someone who engaged in resolute sacrifice for a covenant encounter with the Lord. Many of us are familiar with Abraham's sacrificial obedience. Abraham's unflinching faithfulness to the Lord is a worthy example for every generation. Indeed, he was desperate to please the Lord and to align himself with the Lord's dictates. His only son Isaac, his very precious possession, was demanded by the Lord to be offered as a sacrifice. But as tough and challenging as this demand by God appeared, Abraham still obeyed! By virtue of his desperate obedience, the Lord made an unending relational covenant with him, which made him overflow in blessings and become a channel of blessing to many generations. Once you are desperate to have a deep relationship with God, you would give whatever it takes to achieve it. Those who are emboldened by grace to give up their possessions and positions for the manifestation of God's covenant and God's glory, always get the fullness of God's riches.

What position do you currently occupy that is too great to give up for a covenant encounter with God? What position still pins you to the world and separates you from God? I still consider it ridiculous to reach for earthly positions at the expense of divine placement. God is the Controller of Heaven and earth. We didn't create ourselves, God created you and I for His pleasure; hence, you should live for Him, live to please Him and worship Him. Revelation 4:11 says, "Thou art worthy, O Lord, to receive glory and honor and power, because thou hast created all things, and for thy pleasure, they are and were created." We were created for His pleasure! You should be ever willing to sacrifice your treasure for His pleasure and your time for His testimony. No material possession and earthly position are too much to give up just to please the Lord. Without God, we are nothing and we must be ready to give up anything and everything to please Him. The only way to see the performance of the Lord's promises over our lives as embedded in the Scriptures is to please the Lord. There is no other way but this! When you give up your positions and possessions to please God, God Himself would take you up. He will establish a covenant of peace and joy with you and make you a wonder to your generation and to generations to come.

Negligence in the place of sacrificial obedience to the Lord always causes spiritual shallowness. No man can be deep in the Spirit if he doesn't exhibit the habit of sacrificial obedience to the Lord. Those who want to go deep in the love and covenant of God must be willing to please God sacrificially. It is egregious to exempt yourself from a sacrificial service to the glory of your Maker, you will be doing yourself a great disservice by so doing. Whosoever gives sacrificially to our eternal Lord, would have eternal peace, eternal joy, and eternal life. Giving of tithes, giving of first fruits, giving of offerings and other sacrificial giving for the furtherance of the gospel of Christ are tangible examples of sacrificial obedience to God. You won't struggle with paying your tithe if you're mindful or desirous of a covenant relationship with God. If you cannot honor the Lord with your substance, you cannot harvest His covenant blessings. When you sow seeds of sacrifice to the Lord, you reap showers of blessings. Sacrifice is the benchmark for getting covenant blessings from God. In 1kings chapter 3, we find the account of King Solomon, who attained the height of overflowing prosperity, exceeding peace, and supernatural wisdom because he sacrificially offered a thousand burnt offering. This very rare sacrificial act of Solomon provoked God into doing the unusual. God gave him an open check and blessed him with uncommon wisdom. Isn't it mind-blowing to have God give you an open check? What an enormous grace! But this grace came by sacrifice. Solomon offered one thousand of his choice animal possessions. What a sacrifice! God will be moved by such a gross act of sacrifice. It was a miracle-provoking and destiny-glorifying sacrifice. It is crucial for us to know that God still demands this kind of sacrifice from us. Let's see what the Bible says about David and the Israelites as regards their routine offer of sacrifices to the Lord: "And David said to all the congregation, now bless the Lord your God. And all the congregation blessed the Lord God of our fathers, and bowed down their heads and worshipped the Lord and the King.

And they sacrificed sacrifices unto the Lord and offered a burnt offering unto the Lord, on the morrow after that day, even a thousand lambs, with their drink offerings and sacrifices in abundance for all Israel. 1Chronicles 29:20-21

The connotation of the above Scriptural passage is that David and the children of Israel had a culture of and a standard for offering sacrifices to God. It was their way of activating and renewing their covenant with the Lord. Presumably, Solomon offered a thousand offerings because he learned by culture, that David and the children of Israel offered a thousand lambs as a sacrifice to the Lord. Perhaps, Solomon wanted to continue the standard and provoke God to locate him with wondrous virtues that'll make him stand out. Do not undermine the power of sacrificial giving under any condition. Though the road may be rough and the situation may be tough, yet, key into giving sacrificially to the Lord and be rest assured that you will see the speedy miraculous move of God over your life. The Lord empowers a sacrificial giver to become a glory-carrier and a wonder-commander after the order of Solomon. The Lord's amazing response to Solomon's sacrifice remains the disposition He would manifest towards your sacrifice also. We know this because Hebrews 13:8 tells us that "Jesus Christ is the same yesterday, the same today and the same forever." In the place of covenant transactions, God still rates sacrifices of our possessions and positions very highly and He responds to them very promptly. God honors sacrifices offered to Him in unhampered submission, unfeigned willingness, undefiled consecration, unwavering faith and unreserved dedication.

As earlier established, our sacrifices to God constantly activate, fuel, maintain, and renew our covenant relationship with God. The degree of your sacrifice determines the depth of your relationship with the Lord. Always remember that we are children of the lineage of Abraham and to attract the Abrahamic order of blessings, we must offer Abraham's kind of sacrifices. Give up your best to the Lord!

Why Sacrifice for Him?

Since God sacrificially sent His only begotten Son to the world to die for our sins and redeem us by His precious blood that was shed, we are expected by covenant to reciprocate His sacrifice by sacrificing for Him too. "He, Himself is the sacrifice that atones for our sins—and not only our sins but the sins of all the world" – 1John 2:2. Jesus Christ the Son of God, the Atonement for our sins sacrificed His life for us by His death on the cross of Calvary in order to reconcile us with God. His death brought us salvation, His resurrection brought justification to our faith. The onus is therefore on us to engage the redemptive sacrifice of Christ for our profiting by giving ourselves as a living, holy and acceptable sacrifice to Him in return. Our commitment to Him demands a sacrifice! "He died for everyone so that those who receive His new life will no longer live for themselves. Instead, they will live for Christ, who died and was raised for them" – 1Corinthians 15:2.

No great relationship can be established without a sacrifice; sacrifice strengthens the cords of friendship and lengthens its span. When sacrifice is engaged with the Son of God, everlasting life with God is encountered. We know this because John 3: 16 says, "...whosoever believes in Him would not perish but have everlasting life." An intimate relationship with God through Jesus Christ the Son ultimately leads to everlasting life in unspeakable joy and glorious peace. But this can only be established and activated on the platform of sacrifice.

How would you sacrifice for God in order to establish a thriving relationship with Him? David, the man after God's heart, who had a great relationship with God, gave us some insights into the God kind of sacrifice in Psalm 51:17&19a, which says, "The sacrifices of God are a broken spirit, a broken and a contrite heart, O God, you will not despise. Then will You delight in right sacrifices." Our Lord delights in sacrifices done with a broken or lowly, or surrendered heart. Brokenness is one of the surest keys to Kingdom fullness and fruitfulness. No one can flourish with the Lord without having a broken spirit and a penitent heart. Isaiah 62:10 reveals that we are Holy People, the Redeemed of the Lord, sought out and a city not forsaken. But these Kingdom positions cannot be attained until we exhibit absolute submission to the Lord in brokenness and penitence.

The Rewards for Kissing the Son

As we proceed, I would like you to retain in your heart the KISS we've expounded in chapter 1 to chapter 4, which is the key to an intimate and flourishing covenant relationship with God. **K-Keep His laws, I – Interact with Him, S – Study His Words**, and **S- Sacrifice for Him**. As simple as these guides may seem, they are the incisive covenant guides for the establishment of a flourishing covenant relationship with the Lord. Furthermore, we will be considering the tremendous rewards of kissing the Son in the subsequent chapters and establish these rewards with simplicity. In light of these, let's consider the letters of the word **"SON"**.

Kiss The Son

A Guide To A Flourishing and Intimate Covenant Relationship with God

CHAPTER 5

S - SUCCESS ON EVERY SIDE

One of the essences of kissing the Son of God - Jesus Christ our Lord is to attract His virtues which would propel us to attain great heights of success on every side. When you kiss the Son, He empowers you to succeed on every side. This eternal truth is expressly revealed in the Book of Joshua 1:8, which says, "Study this Book of Instruction continually. Meditate on it day and night so you will be sure to obey everything written in it. Only then shall you prosper and *succeed in all you do."*

All round success becomes your lot once you plant a kiss on the Son. We need not look for success anywhere else, all that we need is in Jesus. By kissing Him- Jesus, we are connecting to the Spirit of God in Him, which is the Spirit of success. The virtues of success abundantly abound in the Son. He is the Custodian of every virtue and we are positioned to draw from His abundant virtues when we draw near to Him. The woman with the issue of blood in Luke 8:43-48, came in close contact with Him after pressing hard to touch Him by faith, and she was able to draw from the abundant healing virtues in the Son, which terminated her health woes and established the success of her health. Apparently, she had spent all her living on physicians, but her health failures continued until she touched the Great Physician – Jesus Christ. The Son of God will supply all your needs if you could surrender to His will. And as we earlier stated in the preamble of this book, His earnest will is to have an intimate relationship with you. Let Jesus feel your touch, just as He felt the touch of the woman. Until you touch Him, you cannot attract His virtues, and His virtues empower you to succeed. The virtues in Jesus Christ are powerful enough to terminate every crisis in your life. Just kiss Him, let Him feel your touch, and your success will be evident to all. In verse 46, Jesus, speaking concerning the woman with the issue of blood said, "Somebody hath touched me: for I perceive that virtue is gone out of me." We can justifiably infer from this passage that the only way we can tap into the virtues of Jesus Christ is touching Him. In our context, we are to touch the Lord with our KISS. According to God's Word, the Lord God is a Spirit, hence, we can only touch the Lord through the things of the Spirit which have been fully revealed to us in the word KISS. So whenever you kiss the Son, you touch the Son, and whenever you touch the Son, virtues flow out of Him to you, which would make you an embodiment of success. His virtues give physical and spiritual stamina. By reason of His virtues, you will not fall nor fail, you will not be weary and will not faint.

Success in the Son

No one can experience success in the Son without a deliberate and conscious effort to remain or continue steadfastly in an intimate relationship with Him. In your journey through life, success can only be established when you abide in the Lord. Success becomes your portion when you are deliberate and definitive in your relationship with Him. You don't experience success in the Lord by accident, you experience success in the Lord by being deliberate, devoted and diligent.

The woman with the issue of blood touched Him deliberately. She was deliberate and desperate for a close contact with the Son, and this led to the manifestation of her success. She approached the Son deliberately and desperately, and He terminated her reproach. As your appetite for kissing the Son is being activated via the insights in this book, may the Lord terminate every reproach in your life and turn your failures into successes in Jesus' Name.

Sometimes, the Lord wants to see your desperation before you can see His intervention. The subject of desperation as regards our relationship with God should be magnified in the body of Christ. This is because those who seek the Lord diligently and in desperation for an encounter with Him, always get the intervention of the Lord, which culminates in their celebration.

Are you desperate for an encounter with the Son? Are you desperate for His intervention in that ugly and unpleasant situation? If yes, you need to engage in great faith and a prayer of desperation. The prayer of desperation engenders speedy divine intervention. Upon living a life of frustrations and failures, Jabez prayed a prayer of desperation to the Lord and his situation was changed into good success. "He was the one who prayed to the God of Israel, 'Oh that You would bless me and expand my territory! Please be with me in all that I do and keep me from all trouble and pain!' And God granted him his request"- 1Chronicles 4:10. Let's adopt this as a model for the prayer of desperation. We can decode from Jabez' prayer that he was in dire need of a transformation and divine intervention. Beloved, the manifestation of your all-around success hinges on your desperation for divine intervention. By Heaven's intervention, our success is guaranteed. Nehemiah said, "The God of Heaven will help us succeed..." Nehemiah 2:20.

If you desire divine encounter, you're required of the Lord to pray a prayer of desperation in faith. Success on every side can only be guaranteed when you have a relationship with the Lord. It has been established in God's Word that the Lord knows those who are His, and He grants their desires, but the prayer of a sinner is an abomination to the Lord. Proverbs 10:24 says, "The fear of the wicked, it shall come upon him: but the desires of the righteous shall be granted." You must command the presence of God before you can boldly place a demand on the Throne of Grace. By reason of this, we need to be righteous! As we remain in right standing with the Lord, He would stand up for us and empower us for success all-around.

More so, continuity in your relationship with the Lord is key to continual success. You need to continue with Him in loyalty, faithfulness, firmness, steadfastness and unwavering commitment. As you do this, you will succeed more and more until His Kingdom comes.

Kiss The Son

A Guide To A Flourishing and Intimate Covenant Relationship with God

CHAPTER 6

O - OVERFLOWING JOY, PEACE, AND POWER

Overflowing Joy

Another benefit we derive from planting a KISS on the SON is overflowing joy, this is the greatest level of joy. When your joy overflows, it becomes transmissible. It extends to others and decorates their destinies beautifully. Jesus Christ the Son of God is the Custodian of this kind of joy, and He only makes it available to those who KISS Him. Jesus Christ is the Joy of the world! He brought salvation to the world, thereby bringing the joy that overflows. The joy was extended to mankind from generations to generations, but it can only be activated by accepting Him as Lord and Savior and by planting a KISS on Him.

Overflowing joy is a complete joy. It is a joy that is full of glory. We attract this kind of joy by believing the Son and kissing the Son. Let's garner more understanding on overflowing joy. 1Peter 1:8 says, "Whom having not seen, ye love; in whom, though now ye see Him not, yet believing, ye rejoice with joy unspeakable and full of glory." Considering the Spirit-filled words of Peter in this passage, we can establish that those who KISS the Son of God because they love Him and believe wholeheartedly in Him, would rejoice with joy unspeakable and full of glory. Overflowing joy is literally unexplainable and it is characterized by glory. It is a great reward for those who love the Lord and those who KISS Him passionately.

Overflowing joy also extends into eternity. It is a joy that is more than sufficient to last you forever – everlasting joy. Everlasting joy is the portion of the redeemed. Everlasting joy is the portion of the ransomed. Anyone who is not connected to the Cross of Calvary cannot manifest everlasting joy. It is the joy that is reserved for those who KISS the Son. Isaiah 51:11 says, "Therefore, the redeemed of the Lord shall return, and come with singing unto Zion; and everlasting joy shall be upon their head: they shall obtain gladness and joy, and sorrow and mourning shall flee away."

The moment you attain the status of the redeemed, you activate everlasting joy upon your head. Since your head is the symbol of your glory, it, therefore, means that once you've been redeemed by the Lord, everlasting joy is activated upon your glory. No wonder Peter described this joy as joy unspeakable and full of glory. Oh, what a glorious joy!

May this overflowing joy become your portion as you KISS the Son, in the mighty Name of Jesus.

Overflowing Peace

The peace that overflows is described by the Bible as peace like a river. Prophet Isaiah speaking in Isaiah 66:12a says, "For thus saith the Lord, Behold, I will extend peace to her like a river." Overflowing peace is a great reward for kissing the Son. Everyone who has been redeemed by the Lord and has a covenant relationship with Him has been called to Peace. Apostle Paul, while speaking by the Holy Spirit's leading to the

Colossian Church enlightened and admonished us to let the peace of Christ rule in our hearts, since as members of one body we've been called to peace. Colossians 3:15

Overflowing peace is the peace of God that surpasses all understanding. It is an unfathomable peace. Philippians 4:7 says, "Then you will experience God's peace, which exceeds anything we can understand. His peace will guard your hearts and minds as you live in Christ Jesus." The Lord has promised us peace that overflows as long as we remain in Him. Our Lord is the Custodian of peace. According to Isaiah 9:6, He is the Prince of Peace. Therefore, endeavor to place yourself righteously in His will, in order to be a carrier of His overflowing peace.

Overflowing Power

Empowerment from above is a blessing that comes with having a relationship with the Son. Overflowing power comes when you KISS the Son. Overflowing anointing comes when you KISS the Lord. Divine empowerment is a function of divine connection. If you are not connected to God by covenant, you cannot attract the overflowing power of God. It is expressly revealed in the Scripture that all power in Heaven and earth belongs to God. David said, "God hath spoken once; twice have I heard this; that power belongeth unto God." Psalm 62:11

Our Lord is the Almighty and All-powerful. He is committed to bestowing His power upon His vessels. Those who wait on and hold onto the Lord, receive His overflowing Power. God will inject His Power into you when you KISS His Son. In obedience to the Lord's instruction, the disciples of Jesus Christ waited prayerfully to be endued with Power from on high. These disciples had been with the Lord, and they maintained their relationship with Him. They Kissed Him faithfully, so He promised them in Acts 1:8 that they would receive Power after the Holy Spirit comes upon them. The Power of the Holy Spirit is the power of God that overflows. The carrier of this power would command signs, wonders, and prosperity. Furthermore, due to the fact that he/she is operating in overflowing power, he/she would become a channel of blessings to others. Overflowing power isn't just for the benefit of the carrier, but also for those who come in contact with the carrier. It is a power that overflows. It is a power that transcends generations if consciously maintained in righteousness. David attracted this kind of power from the Lord and he never lost any battle. No wonder he said to the Lord, "You prepare a feast for me in the presence of my enemies. You honor me by anointing my head with oil. My cup overflows with blessings" Psalm 23:5. The oil in this context symbolizes power. So we can invariably say that God anointed David with power and the power overflowed. We can also establish evidently that the power continued to flow in the lineage of David, even till the birth of Jesus and beyond. Mind you, Jesus Christ came from the lineage of David and by virtue of this, He was called the Son of David; Revelation 22:16.

God also anointed Jesus Christ with the Holy Spirit and with Power. Our Lord Jesus by the Holy Spirit also extended that divine power to his disciples as we saw earlier.

"And you know that God anointed Jesus of Nazareth with the Holy Spirit and with power. Then Jesus went around doing good and healing all who were oppressed by the devil, for God was with him" Acts 10:38.

The anointing of overflowing power enabled Jesus Christ to prosper in His earthly ministry. The power of God positions you for a wealthy life, a healthy life and a blessed life. According to Deuteronomy 8:18, it is God who gives us the power to make wealth. Cling to the Lord! You need the anointing of overflowing power to fulfill your God-given destiny after the order of Jesus. But you cannot attract this power if you refuse to KISS the Son. I admonish you to covet overflowing power from the Lord and contact it by kissing Him.

As covenant children of God, the Lord has reserved rare powers for you and me to manifest brightly and gloriously as the light of the world and the salt of the earth to the glory of His holy Name. The Lord spoke to me audibly about this agenda on the 28th day of February 2017. The Lord made me know that He has reserved great and yet to be seen power for those who will dedicatedly consecrate themselves to His service and to the course of the gospel in this end-time. The Scripture corroborates this divine information in 1Corinthians 2:9: "But as it is written: Eye hath not seen, nor ear heard, neither have entered into the heart of man, the things which God hath prepared for them that love Him." Unusual power for uncommon exploits is reserved for addicted lovers of God. As we approach the end of time, the Lord is willing to make you a vessel of overflowing power or overflowing anointing if you would just KISS Him. KISS the Son, and He would baptize you with overflowing power. The Lord wants you to be a possessor of overflowing power, which would make you an agent of salvation, an agent of redemption, an agent of reconciliation, an agent of illumination, and an agent of transformation.

Kiss The Son

A Guide To A Flourishing and Intimate Covenant Relationship with God

CHAPTER 7

N – NEVER ENDING GRACE

Once you are in the place of grace with the Lord, lines will fall in pleasant places for you. Grace in this context is the manifestation of divine favor, divine help, divine love, and divine mercy. It is the affectionate and redemptive gift of God to mankind. The grace of God redeems, rescues, restores, revives, renews, refreshes, reconciles, and revitalizes. The height of never-ending grace is the highest and most sublime height you can ever attain as a believer in Christ Jesus, and you can only get there when you KISS the Son. A man whose life is characterized by never-ending grace experiences ceaseless multiplication of God's marvelous and matchless grace upon his life and destiny. Grace is the uncommon, unusual and unmerited favor of God. Mary the mother of Jesus, found this kind of favor with God. "Don't be afraid, Mary," the angel told her, "for you have found favor with God! Luke 1:30.

Mary was a vessel that attracted grace by her righteousness, for she was a virgin – not immoral or unholy; and by reason of this, the Lord used her as the vessel through which His Son was made manifest. This shows us that we cannot exude grace if we are not carriers of grace. It is established in the Scriptures that Jesus Christ is the grace of God. Jesus is Grace Himself! Titus 2:11 says "For the grace of God has been revealed, bringing salvation to all people."

Of course, Jesus Christ brought salvation to the world by shedding His precious blood for us on the Cross. "In whom we have redemption through His blood, the forgiveness of sins, according to the riches of His grace." Ephesians 1:7

Our redemption from damnation and forgiveness of sins was made possible by the riches of the grace of our Lord. His grace is never ending because His precious blood which was shed for the remission of our sins is always available to whosoever desires to be redeemed. While the world remains, the redemptive grace of our Lord will never end. The rhythmic, refreshing and replenishing flow of grace is our portion through Christ's work of redemption.

God will bestow upon us the never-ending grace of His Son, only if we KISS the Son.

Noah upheld his relationship with God in righteousness and found grace with God and his entire household were redeemed from destruction and even animals were preserved. Never ending grace redeems and preserves continually, it exceeds human calculations and extends into generations. Never ending grace is exceeding grace, sufficient and sustaining grace. "And He said unto me, "My grace is sufficient for thee: for my strength is made perfect in weakness. Most gladly, therefore, will I rather glory in my infirmities, that the power of Christ may rest upon me." 2Corinthains 12:9. The Lord has assured us by His word, that on the platform of our covenant relationship with Him, He would give us sufficient grace which is able to sustain us till the glorious day of His appearing. As long as we remain in the will of God, His grace over us will never end! But when we severe our connectivity with the Trinity through sin, grace will be withdrawn. Apostle Paul said, "What shall we say then? Shall we continue in sin, that grace may abound? God forbid. How shall we, that are dead to sin, live any longer therein?" Romans 6:1-2. Sin deactivates and halts the never-ending grace of God in our lives. Let us consciously avoid sin! Beloved, you can only attract the never-ending grace of God through your intimacy with the Lord. In Genesis chapter 6, we find the account of Noah. Noah found this grace in the sight of the Lord, and from his generation till this present generation, the world is still basking in the covenant that God established through His never-ending grace with Noah. The Lord enacted His unending commitment to this Covenant with the sign of the rainbow. Any time we see this sign, we know that grace still abounds. He covenanted never to destroy the world with water again, and this became a reality because Noah found grace in the eyes of the Lord. The never-ending grace that manifested upon Noah has preserved mankind from his generation to date.

Never ending grace provokes increasing greatness. David was a carrier of grace who coveted this, and thus prayed, "Thou shalt increase my greatness and comfort me on every side." Psalm 71:21

Note that David was already a king when he said this prayer. However, his greatness manifested when he was a teenager after he defeated and destroyed Goliath. But even as a king, he still aspired for more greatness. Nothing great is achieved by age, everything great is achieved by grace. All you need is the Son of God by your side at all times, for by Him all grace abounds and unending grace avails. Note: for your greatness to continually increase, your grace must be unending.

Never-ending grace also provokes great glory. It is a surpassing grace that launches you into the glory of the latter which is greater than the former – Haggai 2:9. This grace enables you to overtake those who've gone before you. It also enables you to gloriously surpass your own expectation and the expectation of others regarding your destiny. A colorful destiny is made manifest by the never-ending grace of God.

The last sentence of most books usually reflects the central theme of the book. It is quite interesting and edifying to know that the last sentence in the Bible which encapsulates the totality of the Bible is a pointer to the indispensability of grace. It says. "The grace of our Lord Jesus Christ be with you all. Amen." Revelations 22:21

May the Lord bestow His never-ending grace upon your destiny and make your greatness evident to all in Jesus' mighty Name. Amen.

Kiss The Son

A Guide To A Flourishing and Intimate Covenant Relationship with God

CHAPTER 8

KISS THE SON

Kisses are passionate! When you KISS the Son, you're pouring out your passion to Him; and as you pour out your passion to Him, He'll pour out His Spirit upon you. "In the last days,' God says, 'I will pour out of my Spirit upon all people. Your sons and your daughters will prophesy. Your young men will see visions and your old men will dream dreams" Acts 2:17. The Lord wants us to KISS Him with every ounce of passion in us. To Kiss Him passionately is to Kiss Him wholeheartedly – with all your heart. Every service rendered to the Lord must be rendered from the heart if we want rewards. Passion is good. It is the reflection of our affection towards a person or thing. Jesus Christ was a Man of passion. His passion engendered our redemption from crisis, calamities, and condemnation. Another way of connecting with the passion of Christ is eating and drinking the Holy Communion. As often as we eat and drink the Holy Communion in remembrance of Him, we connect with His passion, thus getting His Spirit's fullness – 1Corinthians 11:24-25.

When you KISS the Son, you lean on Him. You can't engage in a deep KISS with your hands or body not resting on the person you are kissing. When you lean on Him, He gives you rest. Jesus said in Matthew 11:28, "come to me, all of you who are weary and carry heavy burdens, and I will give you rest," When you lean on the Lord, He'll give you all-round rest.

❖ **Kiss the Son no matter who is watching and no matter what is happening**: Kiss Him against all odds, against all antagonism, against all discouragements, and against all trials. The Son forewarned us in John 16:33, He said, "I have told you all this so that you may have peace in me. Here on earth, you will have many trials and sorrows. But take heart, because I have overcome the world." By the words of our Lord, we are to remain cheerful and full of faith even in the midst of the storms of life. Our disposition towards seemingly unpleasant situations should be positive because our Lord has overcome the world for us. No matter what anyone says or does, we should remain focused on Him. See these striking words in Songs of Solomon 8:1b: "then I could kiss you no matter who was watching." We are to Kiss the Son at all times, no matter who is watching, and no matter who said what, when, and from whom. This is because the moment you take your eyes off the Lord and your lips off His Lips, you open the door to the devil and to destruction. Never let go of the presence of the Lord! Hold on tenaciously to Him. The devil is always seeking to break your relationship with the Lord. He is looking diligently for whom to devour. He knows that your strength and safety is in the Lord. Therefore, refuse to let go of God. Hold on steadfastly to Him. Look constantly unto the Author and Finisher of your faith. Cling earnestly and continually to the old-rugged cross. You must guard your relationship with the Lord jealously, with all diligence, watchfulness, and prayerfulness. You mustn't allow anyone or anything to separate you from the Love of God. Kiss the Son till His Kingdom comes.

❖ **Kiss the Son without the fear of men**: The Lord expects us to always engage the fear of God in order to continually kiss the Son. God is not glorified when we put the fear of men above Him. He is always disappointed whenever we please men rather than please Him. God must be honored above the dictates of men! King Saul ended up in desolation because he aligned himself with the dictates of men. He allowed the words of men to overrule the Words of God. See Saul's disparaging statement in 1Samuel 15:24, "And Saul said unto Samuel, I have sinned: for I have transgressed the commandment of the Lord, and thy words: because I feared the people, and obeyed."

Beloved, do not tie your destiny to human promises and dictates, especially if they aren't in consonance with the Word and perfect will of God. Humans will fail you, but God never fails! So don't rely on people, rely on God. Repose your trust and confidence in God alone. If you fear the Lord indeed, He will never fail you! He will also raise destiny helpers for you, who will help you sacrificially without fail. The best way to come into favor with the Lord is to fear Him.

"Then Peter and the other apostles answered and said, we ought to obey God rather than men" Acts 5:29. If you say you are a believer, then you must have the guts to stand against what God is against. Standards of the world must not override the standard of the Word. Global reality must never supersede Scriptural reality. You must not tolerate what the Word of God does not accommodate. Christianity entails absolute submission and commitment to the will of God. The Lord needs your loyal, firm, steadfast, unmovable and unwavering commitment. Don't put your life on the back burner of planting a KISS on the Son, put your life right in God's Kingdom by kissing the Son. Jesus Christ our Lord made a thought-provoking statement in Luke 12:5. He said, "But I'll tell you whom to fear. Fear God, who has the power to kill you and then throw you into hell. Yes, He's the One to fear." God is the One to fear, not men. God always rescue and redeem those who fear Him from destruction. Joseph was a man who feared God. He rejected the immoral advances of Potiphar's wife and he affirmed this through his righteous response to her, borne out of the fear of God. He said, "No one here has more authority than I do. He has held back nothing from me except you because you are his wife. How could I do such a wicked thing? It would be a great sin against God." Anyone that fears the Lord and wants to continually KISS the Son, would always speak in this manner in the face of any temptation. Consequently, elevation or promotion manifests for that person's celebration. After Joseph overcame that temptation, the Lord caused him to be elevated and celebrated in the land of Egypt. In view of Joseph's temptation, we can rightly establish that the fear of God is the panacea for temptation. As long as the fear of God is retained in your heart, your lips and your totality would remain attached to the Lord and Kingdom romance would continue. Let the fear of God rule your life so that your relationship with God would flourish, even into eternal life.

Many have rejected the glorious and wonderful opportunity to get into an intimate relationship with God because of what people will say. They fear being persecuted; they fear being called untoward names. If you are truly in Love with the Lord, you wouldn't care about what people say, all you'll care about is His all-consuming and richly-rewarding presence. Remember, no one will answer your questions for you on the Day of Judgment, therefore, let no man prevent you from kissing the Lord. Go all out for Him, let the zeal for His house consume you, KISS Him like never before and let God approve you. Whatever God approves nobody can disapprove. Men's approval won't make you the apple of God's eyes, will not get you to be associated with divinity, and will not attract the attention of the Trinity to you. Seek to be approved unto God through the thorough study of His Word according to 2Timothy 2:15. Seek the status of divine approval, for your intimacy with God hinges on this. I still remember the expression of orgasmic excitement on my face when I heard the Lord approve of me in 2013, by these words: "The Big Wow!" Since then, I've been catapulted by grace to great heights in the Lord with signs following.

Beloved, there cannot be a manifestation of intimacy with God if the Lord does not approve of you. Once the status of divine approval is attained, intimacy with the Lord is gained.

God is so sweet to serve, but you cannot enjoy the sweetness of God until you KISS the Son.

"Let us hear the conclusion of the whole matter: Fear God, and keep His commandments: for this is the whole duty of man" Ecclesiastes 12:13.

❖ **Kiss the Son Faithfully**: Faithfulness is required in our relationship with the Son. There is no unfaithfulness in our Lord, and because we have been redeemed by His blood and indwelled by His Spirit to be like Him, He doesn't want to find unfaithfulness in us. The relationship we have with the Son by covenant is likened to that of a bride/wife and a bridegroom/husband. According to the Scripture, we are His bride and He is the bridegroom; and He demands utmost faithfulness from us so that when He comes to receive us unto Himself, He would meet us without spot, wrinkle or blemish – Ephesians 5:25-27. Let us remain faithful to our Lord. Let us uphold our integrity even as we engage dutifully in our covenant relationship with Him. Let's not be like Judas, who kissed Him unfaithfully and ended up in perdition, desolation, and destruction. Judas planted a kiss of betrayal on our Lord! This is gross unfaithfulness at work. We understand by Scriptures that Judas Iscariot the betrayer identified Jesus Christ by a prearranged signal of a kiss. This is an unfaithful and unholy kiss. It is a kiss borne out of covetousness, love of money and unrighteousness. In 2Corinthians 13:12, Apostle Paul, enjoins us believers to greet one another with a holy kiss, not with a deceptive or destructive kiss. A holy kiss is a kiss of love – agape love. Don't be like Judas the betrayer, be like Jesus the Lover of our soul. Be faithful in your relationship with the Lord of your life and great will be your rewards. You must give the Lord your loyal devotion before He approves you as a royal priesthood. When your loyalty to the Lord is undivided, your blessings are unlimited. Until you serve the Lord faithfully, you will not get His blessings optimally. The Lord takes pleasure in those who honor Him, in those who adore and celebrate Him faithfully. Honor the Son, and by so doing you are honoring the Father. One of the coherent assertions of this undying truth comes in the Book of John 5:3, where Jesus Christ expressly said, "So that everyone will honor the Son, just as they honor the Father. Anyone who does not honor the Son is certainly not honoring the Father who sent Him." Furthermore, the Almighty God, speaking through His prophet Samuel in 1Samuel 2:30b, says, "... But I will honor those who honor me, and I will despise those who think lightly of me. Beloved, I assure you that God will honor you if you serve Him honorably, and God will not fail you if you serve Him faithfully. Faithfulness to God culminates in fruitfulness in life. It is central to a flourishing relationship with God. The Lord desires and demands that you commit to Him uncompromisingly. If you want to see the actuality of God's promises for your life, you must resolve never to compromise your faith. Unwavering faithfulness to the Lord gets you to your promise land.

The Son is Always Seeking to Kiss You

Jesus Christ our Lord and Savior, the Son of the Most High God, is always seeking to kiss you and me. He craves an intimate relationship with us. He said, "Behold, I stand at the door and knock: if any man hear my voice, and open the door, I will come in to him and sup with him and he with me" Revelations 3:20. Let's look at this amazing statement keenly. Our Lord reveals in this statement that He is a relational God. He is seeking a close and cordial relationship with you. He is right at the door of your heart knocking and hoping that you would open your heart to Him and welcome Him into your life, in order to have a flourishing relationship with Him. He wants to be close to you, and He wants you to be close to Him. He wants to walk with you while you walk with Him. He wants to live in you while you live in Him. He wants to abide in you while you abide in Him. He wants to kiss you while you kiss Him. I urge you to give the Son of God the right of way in your life and resist the devil's crafty schemes to lure you into an evil relationship with him.

Our Father and our Lord is always seeking to kiss us, even when we are far away from Him due to the pleasure of sin. We were created for His pleasure and not for His pain. He is our Potter and we are the clay. He made us solely to manifest His purpose, which is to be closely knitted with Him by covenant. Therefore, until intimacy with God is accomplished on earth, life has no meaning. A life of meaning is a life that is in tandem with the Potter's purpose. Not all rich men are living a meaningful life. Being rich does not equal being in the center of God's will, neither does being a rich man equal fulfillment of life's purpose. A meaningful life is a covenant life in God and a relational life with the Lord. It's high time you stopped existing and start living according to the Potter's purpose.

The disposition of the father of the prodigal son when his son returned home is a true reflection of our Heavenly Father's disposition to us whenever we return to Him in penitence. We find the account in Luke 15:20: "So he returned home to his father. And while he was still a long way off, his father saw him coming. Filled with love and compassion, he ran to his son, embraced him, and kissed him." Our God is a jealous and compassionate God. He is seeking an intimate relationship with us and He does not desire that any should perish, but that all should come to repentance. Let's make ourselves available for the blessed Kiss of our Father.

The devil, your archenemy is also seeking to kiss you with the kiss of deception, destruction, and damnation. Don't let him plant a kiss of darkness on your lips. The devil's core desire is to break your relationship with God. Proverbs 27:6 reveals that the kisses of an enemy are deceitful, and 1Peter 5:8 reveals that our enemy, the devil is prowling around like a roaring lion, looking for someone to devour or destroy. According to John 10:10, the devil has a 3 fold ministry: which is to steal joy, kill glory and destroy destiny. But if you refuse to let him into your heart, refuse to allow him to rule over your life and refuse to let the devil kiss you, then his evil ministry will never prosper over your life and destiny. May the Lord give you the grace to keep the devil perpetually out of your life in Jesus' Name.

Beloved, you can't afford to kiss the devil even for a moment, for that will be a great error that one may never recover from. The devil has no power over you if you don't give him the right of way in your life. Therefore, shut the door of your heart permanently to the devil. Turn your eyes away from the enticing, ephemeral and mundane things of this world, which are the instruments used by the devil to manipulate and distract. Once your relationship with God or spiritual life starts to wane, the devil gets alerted to attack. Once the things of this world become acceptable to you at the expense of the things of God, you'll become vulnerable to the devil's attack. Therefore my brethren, turn your eyes upon Jesus alone and delight only in the things of God! Focus on kissing the Son of God. Concentrate on Him alone, confide in Him alone, consecrate yourself to Him alone and count on Him alone. Keep your eyes on Jesus and plant your KISS on Him.

When you kiss the Son, your eyes come in contact with His Eyes. By reason of this, you get empowered to see invisible, great and mighty things which you know not. You get empowered to see things with the eyes of God and you become a man of uncommon vision. More so, the visions you get on the platform of kissing the Son would launch you into the realm of miraculous and wondrous manifestations. You will become a wonder to behold by the instrumentality of these visions. Proverbs 29:18 emphasizes the importance of visions. It says, "Where there is no vision the people perish, but he that keepeth the law, happy is he." Divine vision empowers you for divine exploits. Uncommon vision empowers you for uncommon exploits. It is vital to establish that divine and uncommon visions stem from your covenant engagement with Jesus Christ the Son. KISS Him now!

When you KISS the Son – Lord Jesus, He breathes into you. Whenever the act of kissing is activated, there's always an exchange of breath. In this context, the Son takes your breath and puts His breath on you. His breath is the breath of life, the breath of light and the breath of inspiration. He also breathes His Holy Spirit upon us when we kiss Him. Job 32:8 says, "But there is a spirit in man: and the inspiration of the Almighty giveth them understanding." This affirms that the breath of the Lord is the breath of inspiration which gives understanding. We need Scriptural understanding to flourish in our relationship with God. Without understanding, we cannot thrive in life and in the things of the Spirit. David said to the Lord, "The righteousness of thy testimonies is everlasting, give me understanding and I shall live" Psalm 119:114. David understood the power of understanding. He knew that he wouldn't survive and succeed in the battles of life without having an understanding of the mysteries and deep things of God. We also need understanding in this might. Understanding enables you to live an outstanding life. The understanding that comes through the inspiration of the Lord will empower you to live and walk daily in the supernatural. We are enlightened and uplifted by our understanding.

When you kiss the Son, you get divine direction, blessed sanctification, and great glorification after the order of Moses. When you kiss the Son, His face touches your face, and by virtue of this, you attract His glory. The Bible recorded in Exodus 33:11, Exodus 34:30-35, that Moses saw the Lord face to face, and through that encounter, he attracted the glory of the Lord and his face radiated great glory to the awe and amazement of Aaron and the children of Israel. "But we all, with open face beholding as in a glass the glory of the Lord, are changed into the same image from glory to glory, even as by the Spirit of the Lord" 2Corinthians 3:18. Great glorification becomes your lot when you kiss the Son. David the Psalmist declared His Name as the King of Glory. Our Lord is the custodian of glory, and we can only get glorified in Him when we express our love for Him by kissing Him. If your energy is not exerted towards intimacy with God, you will be deserted by God. The worst thing that can ever happen to a man is not physical death, it is to be deserted by God. If you are not fully convinced that God acknowledges you or approves of you, you need to realign yourself with God's will right away and ensure you remain in the center of His will and in right standing with Him. What I fear the most is a disconnection from the Trinity. I don't want to be deserted by my Maker. I don't want to ever hear my Lord say to me, "depart from me, you worker of iniquity." I really fear momentary and eternal separation from God and for this course, I constantly and honestly examine myself to ensure that the Lord is pleased with me and that my rapture status is positive.

I always ask the Lord to reveal my flaws, inconsistencies, and inadequacies to me if there are any; and the Lord always responds by speaking to me, singing to me, revealing a vision to me and showing me a revelation. For this cause, the Lord informs me of temptations to come. He prompts me to restitution, watchfulness, prayerfulness, evangelism, forgiveness, praise, fasting, sacrificial giving, and stewardship. You can do the same and get the same response if you are utterly committed to kissing the Son. Above all things, you should do all it takes to remain connected with the Trinity. This should be your resolve because you are nothing without your Creator.

James declared, "Come close to God, and God will come close to you. Wash your hands, you sinners; purify your hearts, for your loyalty, is divided between God and the world" James 4:8. This Scriptural passage admonishes us to come close to God in the purity of heart and to have undivided or complete loyalty to God. The Spirit of God is calling us to the realization of the importance of absolute loyalty to the Lord. To whom and where is your loyalty? You should be loyal to the Son of God and not to satan. You should be loyal to the Kingdom of light and not to the kingdom of darkness. You should be loyal to the Lord and not to the world. Give the Lord God your loyal devotion! Come under the covering of God now so that you can avoid the sweltering of hell. Let the Lord transform you just as He transformed Saul the persecutor to Paul the preacher. Don't be conformed to the world, but be discrete with the world. You must be discrete with the world if you want to access the secrets of God. Discreteness in the world is one of the keys to greatness in the Kingdom. To be discrete in the world is to be separated from the world. 2Corinthians 6:17 says, "Therefore, come out from among unbelievers and separate yourselves from them, says the Lord. Don't touch their filthy things and I will welcome you." We've been called to render a discrete service to God and that's why we are called 'the church' – people who've been called out of the darkness of the world into the Light of God. We are peculiar people, who are unrelated to the systems, programs, and patterns of the world. We are people who are unequally yoked with unbelievers and we believe in the only true God through Jesus Christ His Son.

When you KISS the Son, you put your trust in Him; putting your trust in the Lord is so rewarding. Psalm 125:1 says, "Those who trust in the Lord are as secure as Mount Zion; they will not be defeated but will endure forever." What a great reward for trusting in the Lord. Inferring from this passage of Scripture, everlasting security, and unending victory is the portion of whosoever puts their trust in the Lord or repose confidence in Him. By this word, the Lord is saying that whosoever kisses His Son will be secured, will never be defeated, and will have eternal life. Jeremiah 17:7 also says: "But blessed are those who trust in the Lord and have made the Lord their hope and confidence." This expressly tells us that the blessings of God come upon a man who puts His trust in the Lord by Kissing the Son.

When you KISS the Son, He launches you into His BLISS. When you obediently serve the Lord, the Lord will cause you to enter into His bliss and joy. In Matthew 25:23, the Lord, while narrating the parable of the three servants, revealed the model of His response and disposition towards those who serve Him faithfully. "Well done, good and faithful servant, thou hast been faithful over a few things, I will make thee ruler over many things: enter thou into the Joy of thy Lord." The connotation to this statement is that the Lord would see to it that His faithful servants or those who KISS Him are elevated to greater heights of glory and share in the treasures, pleasures, and bliss of His Kingdom.

Your prayer should be, "Kiss me oh Lord that I may enter into your bliss." As we indicated in Chapter 2, one of the ways to KISS the Son is by praising Him. When you shower Him with praise, He will shower you with blessings. If you sing His praise always, He would always lift you up. David understood the power of ceaseless praise. David said, "I will bless the Lord at all times, His praise shall continually be in my mouth" Psalm34:1. If you constantly praise God, you will constantly receive from Him. The Lord will intercede for you if you have the habit of praising Him and this intercession will establish eternal glorification for you. On the platform of praise, you have access to divine information that will prevent you from making a destiny-wrecking decision. Kiss Him with praise, for praise works wonders in our covenant relationship with God. In the year 2017, during one of the Holy

Ghost Services held monthly at the Redemption Camp in Nigeria, my Spiritual father, Pastor Enoch Adeboye, while admonishing the congregation on praise, made a wonderful statement that struck me. He said, "If you praise God with all your heart, He would come and Kiss you." He further said admonishingly, "Praise the Lord till He comes and Kisses you." I pondered a lot on this gospel statements thereafter and the Holy Spirit opened my spiritual eyes to the reality and efficacy of this eternal truth. I understood through the inspiration of the Holy Spirit that when you praise God in holiness, you move God to kiss you. Just imagine how great it would be for the Almighty God to come down and literally or spiritually kiss you. It is indeed a blessed imagination. If the Lord kisses you, no one can stop you. The kiss of the Lord would empower you to fulfill His purpose. The kiss of the Lord would place a mark of distinction, protection, exaltation, fortification, and glorification upon you. Provoke the Lord to kiss you by your high praises and great will be your joy.

When you kiss the Son, He would give you the keys to His Kingdom. He promised us affirmatively in Matthew 16:19, saying, "And I will give you the keys of the Kingdom of Heaven. Whatever you forbid on earth will be forbidden in Heaven, and whatever you permit on earth will be permitted in Heaven." The fulfillment of this promise of our Lord hinges on our covenant relationship with Him, which can only be established by kissing the Son. Note: Our Lord was speaking to His disciples or followers in this passage. In the light of this covenant promise, we know for sure that kissing the Son confers dominion. The Lord hands over the keys of dominion and answers to prayers to us on the platform of intimacy with God. By kissing the Son, we have authority to command situations and tides to turn in our favor. In Luke 21:13, the Lord said, "And it shall turn to you for a testimony." When you KISS the Son, you are empowered to become a commander after the order of Jesus Christ, who commanded the stormy wind to be still. I know without an iota of doubt that as you KISS the Son with all your heart, every ugly situation you are going through will turn to you for a testimony in Jesus' Name. More so, Romans 8:28 established that all things work together for good to them that love God and to them who are called according to His purpose." This shows us that as long as we continue to love the Lord and to kiss the Son, all things will work together for our good; but the moment we stop loving the Lord and stop walking according to His purpose for our lives, all things will stop working for our good and this ultimately leads to destruction. Refuse to be set apart from the Trinity. Refuse to be deceived by the devil's antics. Refuse to be defiled by the devil's enticement. Guard your mind by the living word of God from being defiled; because your mind is the seat of wisdom, and once your mind is defiled, your purpose is defeated. Refuse to let the presence of God depart from you. Some time ago, I was in a vision when the Lord said a prayer point to me audibly. He said, "Father, do not let Your presence depart from me." When I woke up from that vision, I prayed this prayer point fervently and I determined in my heart never to let the presence of God depart from me even for a second. I made this determination because the absence of God's presence in a man's life would usher in sorrows. But according to Psalm 16:11, the fullness of Joy is guaranteed in the presence of God. So if we want our joy to continue, we must faithfully and sacrificially ensure that the presence of God is retained in our lives.

We have established earlier via the potency of God's word that our intimate covenant relationship with God must continue if we want the great rewards to remain even in increasing measures. Let's also establish that we will be consumed on earth and eternally in hell if we stop the blessed act of kissing the Son. God is no respecter of persons. As regards our covenant relationship with God, there's no unevenness of consequences. The consequence of sin is death, and this consequence applies to all. Romans 6:23 reveals that the wages of sin is death, but the gift of God is eternal life through Jesus Christ our Lord. The Word of God is immutable, and its immutability cannot thrive on partiality. Whatsoever the Lord has ordered, He is committed to establishing. The Bible made it crystal clear that the soul who sins will die. Every sinner that refuses to repent is bound for eternal death. For this cause, we shouldn't tolerate iniquity, indecency, and indolence. More so, we shouldn't tolerate compromise, contempt, and contamination. We must steer clear of anything that is disgraceful to our covenant calling, and despicable to our covenant God. Give the Lord your unrelenting love and please the Lord consistently with all of you.

It is of utmost significance to establish that daily mercy accrues to us when we continually KISS the Son; and without the mercy of the Lord, we will be consumed – Lamentations 3:22. This is why continuity in our relationship with the Lord cannot be overemphasized. Your resolve as a lover of God should be: "I have decided to follow Jesus, no turning back!" Truly, challenges are inevitable even as we walk with the Lord but our God is a Specialist in turning challenges into channels of blessings. The Lord can turn the plots of your enemy into platforms for your prosperity. You will face challenges, but stay committed to the Lord and you will surely overcome. Beloved, continuity is key to reaping the greatest rewards of fellowship with the Lord. Can the Lord testify to your unending commitment towards kissing Him? What a wonderful testimony this would be! We should desire divine commendation and make our Potter proud! To be registered in Heaven as a Kingdom relative or as joint-heirs with the Son, we must be committed to following the Lord non-stop. Jesus Christ said, "Anyone who puts a hand to the plow and then looks back is not fit for the Kingdom of God" Luke 9:62. Understanding that our Lord desires a daily relational covenant relationship with us is paramount to the continuity of our love for Him and our relationship with Him. God desires truth in the inward parts. He wants us to truthfully, faithfully and diligently maintain a close walk with Him, and not refrain from following Him. Refraining from following the Lord at any given time displeases Him, and it is deciphered as rebellion, and rebellion leads to damnation and destruction. Now that you have put your hand to the 'plow' of service to the Lord through a KISS, please don't look back. When God appoints you to undertake a Kingdom task, you must carry it out without looking back. Remember Lot's wife, who became a pillar of SALT, when she looked back upon disregarding and disobeying the instruction of the Lord. The moment you look back on kissing the Son, you will lose your savor in the Kingdom of God; thereby becoming a vessel unto dishonor. God needs you and me to execute His end-time agenda upon the earth, but we must remain firm in Him and faithful to Him if we would become executors of His glorious purpose. Hebrews 10:38 says, "Now the just shall live by faith: but if any man draws back, my soul shall have no pleasure in him." In this passage, we are admonished not to draw back from the Lord but to draw near to Him. God is grossly displeased and irritated whenever we go back to sinfulness. The moment Lot's wife looked back, she became useless to God's agenda upon the earth. In the same vein, those who withdraw from following the Lord or withdraw from kissing the Son will become a pillar of S- Sorrow, **A**- Affliction, **L**- Limitation, and **T**- Troubles. In 2Timothy 4:10, we find the account of Demas who was a follower of Jesus Christ but deserted the Lord and departed from the faith. By the revealed word of God, I write to you without mincing words that those who are like Demas will end in desolation. Don't be a 'Demas' who forsook the Lord for the mundane and ephemeral things of this world. Because the name Demas means 'popular', I want to believe that he allowed his popularity to separate him from divinity and break his flourishing relationship with the Trinity. Don't be like Demas, be like Daniel who refused to disobey or displease the Lord by defiling himself with the things of the world. Fame and fortune shouldn't stop you from scaling great intimate heights with the Lord. You can be a millionaire and still be meek in submission to God's will. You can be a billionaire and still be a beauty for God. You can be super-righteous and super-rich. You should use everything you have and everything you are to the glory of the Lord. If you have strayed away due to the pleasure of sin, I beseech you by the mercies of God to return to the fold of grace; for it is extremely dangerous to abide outside the conquering-presence of the Almighty. You are only empowered to be more than a conqueror through the great love of Jesus – Romans 8:37. Therefore, don't trade your relationship with God for anything or anyone. Remain on the Lord's side and do not backslide. The moment you gave your life to Jesus Christ, you gave up self-will and you took up God's perfect will. Therefore, don't take back the right of way that you gave to the Lord over your life. A believer must not be given to free will, otherwise, perdition and damnation would befall him. Freedom is only meaningful and acceptable in the Lord. If freedom is not guided, freedom will be perverted! What is the essence of freedom if the Bible is rejected, the dictates of God are despised, and the tenets of the Lord are truncated? Freedom outside the Word and will of God leads to doom. Beloved, there is a drastic difference between freedom in the world and freedom in the Lord. Freedom in the world accommodates abominable and sinful things, while freedom in the Lord only allows holiness and righteousness. As believers, we have been called to freedom in the Lord. John 8:36 expressly says, "So if the Son sets you free, you are free indeed." By virtue of this irrevocable Word, I urge you to claim and maintain your freedom in Christ alone; for freedom in the Son is freedom indeed and in truth, not freedom outside Him. Therefore, don't stop loving the Lord, don't stop serving the living God, don't stop pleasing the Almighty, don't stop obeying your Maker, and don't stop preparing for the second coming of the Lord. Give your all to the Lord and never go back to the world. Let nothing stop you from kissing the Son of God!

Kiss The Son

A Guide To A Flourishing and Intimate Covenant Relationship with God

CHAPTER 9

THE PLACE OF DIVINE ENCOUNTER

One of the greatest benefits of having an intimate relationship with God is a divine encounter. I've discovered by spiritual experiences and by the revelation of Scriptures that it takes divine encounter to make a spiritual giant. Note: Your encounter enables you to counter your enemy. Your encounter empowers you to counter the wiles and devices of the devil. Great destinies are decorated on the platform of divine encounter. Greatness in the gospel cannot be attained without a divine encounter. Divine encounter defines destinies. Any approach to a destiny that doesn't have an attachment to God will end in reproach. Destiny is decorated in the place of divine encounter! The Scripture is a pointer to the timeless truth that the destiny of every Kingdom giant is powered to fulfillment in the place of divine encounter. In Exodus chapter 3, Moses had an encounter with the Lord through the burning bush and the Lord empowered his Rod for signs and wonders. This encounter empowered and emboldened Moses to tackle Pharaoh and triumph over Pharaoh and his hosts. The Bible records that his rod became a snake which swallowed all the snakes of Pharaoh's magicians. Also by his rod, Moses parted the red sea, which climaxed into the destruction of Pharaoh's hosts. We can see that Moses countered the devices, craftiness, and stubbornness of the wicked Pharaoh through his divine encounter. David also had a rare encounter while he was in the field tending to his father's Sheep. The Lord enabled him to kill a Lion and a Bear, and he engaged in this experiential knowledge to defeat Goliath the enemy of Israel. In 1Samuel chapter 17, David confidently countered Goliath through the knowledge of his deliverance encounter with the Lord. He said to Goliath: "This day will the Lord deliver thee into mine hand; and I will smite thee, and take thine head from thee; and I will give the carcasses of the host of the Philistines this day unto the fowls of the air and to the wild beasts of the earth; that all the earth may know that there is a God in Israel. And all this assembly shall know that the Lord saveth not with sword and spear: for the battle is the Lord's, and He will give you into our hands." The Lord empowered the stone in David's hand to destroy his enemy and this culminated in the manifestation of his glory. Beloved, the manifestation of your God-given glory is dependent on your encounters with God. I once had an awesome encounter with Lord, where the Lord sent 3 angels to deliver a message of destiny to me. These angels joyfully, precisely and vocally delivered the information to me and assured me that the Lord will bring His plans for my destiny to fruition. After the angels left, the Lord Himself passed by my side with a speed of light. Immediately I sensed it, I moved with indescribable speed and grabbed Him tightly by His leg, and I said, "Lord, I will not let You go except you pray for me." Then the Lord looked at me, placed His right Hand upon my head and prayed for me. I still remember every word of prayer that He said to me till this day. He disappeared after He had prayed for me and I was full of joy, knowing that I had a Jacob-like encounter. This encounter reinvigorated, revived, renewed and revitalized me spiritually.

The Lord gave me this encounter by grace. However, I played my part in attracting this encounter of grace by planting a KISS on the Son. God is not a respecter of persons; as He gave Moses, David, Jacob, Gideon, and many others from generation to generation divine encounters, God is ever willing to give you a definite encounter if you constantly apply the Kingdom principle – KISS. Whatever God has done for one, He can do for all. Beloved, your background or age does not matter in having a covenant encounter with God. David was a shepherd boy and also a teenager. He wasn't brought up amongst the highs and mighty. He wasn't a full-fletched adult when the Lord located Him by His prophet. He was anointed by God's prophet and separated for glory at a tender age. However, before this glorious encounter, David had always brought joy to the Lord by praising the Lord with instruments and with songs. He had served the Lord relentlessly with meals of praise. He had filled the table of the Lord with precious, acceptable and sweet-smelling dishes of praise. Note: No man is insurmountable; your greatness is determined by what you bring to the Lord's Table. Divine encounter engenders greatness! In the midst of the evident incapability of the old and experienced men of war to terminate the challenger of Israel, David a teenager with an experience of divine encounter confronted and defeated the uncircumcised giant in glorious fashion. Note: Certificates does not certify greatness, serving God does. Energy does not guarantee elevation, encounter does.

David attracted the conquering grace of God through his dedication to giving high praises to the Lord in holiness and righteousness. You can attract it too by planting a KISS on the Lord.

It is an endless truth that divine encounter engenders the manifestation of glory. It is in the place of divine encounter that you get the needed virtues and power to fulfill your God-given destiny in grand style. It is in the place of divine encounter that faulty foundation is repaired and glorious manifestation is revealed. Divine encounter strengthens you and energizes you to exercise great faith in God! As a member of the Army of the Lord, divine encounters would give you experiential and evidential Kingdom messages, which makes the most impact for the cause of the gospel. Seek divine encounter by planting a KISS on the Son! Seek an encounter with the CROSS, where **C** – Comfort and Courage, **R** – Restoration and Redemption, **O** – Overcoming-power and Optimal-blessings, **S** – Satisfaction and Sufficiency, **S** – Salvation and Security flow. There is a 'Rod' and 'Stone' in your hand that the Lord wants to empower for the manifestation of His wonders and glory upon the earth. Just KISS the Son, and the Lord will make you a wonder to your generation and to generations unborn after the order of Abraham, Moses, David, Deborah, and Mary.

God is still in the business of raising end-time Kingdom giants, all He demands is your availability and your commitment to your duty which is to KISS the Son. When you plant a KISS on the Son, you become a Kingdom giant. When you KISS the Son, the devil and his dirty agents will not be able to perform their wicked enterprise against you, every yoke of darkness over you will be broken, the Lord will contend with every contender of your destiny and frustrate the plans of the wicked for your life, every enchantment against your enlargement will fail and every divination against your elevation will be frustrated, generational curses and evil family patterns will be terminated and reversed, every devilish weapon formed against you will not prosper and the devices of the crafty against you will be frustrated, satanic strongholds militating against you will be pulled down, the glory of the Almighty God will overshadow you, you will have access to the Throne of Grace where your demands and desires would be delivered to you, your needs will be supplied and your desires granted, every faulty foundation associated with you will be repaired, you will be delivered from the spirit of errors and mistakes, every negative thing written about you will be erased, you become more than a conqueror, the impossible becomes possible, you begin to reign prosperously and gloriously on earth and reign with Him in glory, and you become glorified with the Father.

May the Lord God visit you as you KISS Him; and may this divine visitation culminate in your elevation and glorification in Jesus' Name.

Kiss The Son

A Guide To A Flourishing and Intimate Covenant Relationship with God

CHAPTER 10

THE PLACE OF DISCIPLINE

It takes discipline to KISS the Son. The role of discipline in establishing and sustaining a flourishing and intimate covenant relationship with God cannot be downplayed. This is because it takes discipline to be a loyal, holy, honorable, and accountable disciple of Jesus Christ the Son. Discipline is the conglomeration of diligence and determination. Discipline must be engaged if destiny is to be encountered and discipline must prevail if your covenant destiny must be preserved. Discipline in kissing the Son must be activated before all blessings as promised by God through his unbreakable covenant with Abraham can be made manifest. A disciplined disciple of Christ has a distinctive character. He doesn't follow the crowd – he stands up for Jesus always and he stands out for God's glory. A disciplined lover of God would pungently and purposefully carry out divine orders, follow divine direction, and walk in divine instruction. An ardent follower of Jesus Christ must embrace discipline in order to fulfill destiny. Discipline defines destiny. The output of your life will be determined by the input of discipline in your life. A lack of discipline in your relationship with God will lead to a loss of intimacy with Him and a disconnection from Heaven. If you want to operate under open Heavens, you must maintain discipline. Discipline in Kissing the Son differentiates a lover of God from a lover of the world. In the things of God, there must be a differentiation before an elevation. "Therefore, come out from among unbelievers, and separate yourselves from them, says the Lord. Don't touch their filthy things, and I will welcome you" – 2Corinthians 6:17. Discipline is what is required to remain separated from the world and remain connected to God. It would equip you to stay in the Lord, and not stray from His fold. Discipline is a display of doggedness in Kingdom service and in your walk with God so that your covenant intimacy with God is maintained. Doggedness is required for experiencing the reality of Kingdom blessedness. It connotes constantly contending for the perfect will and pure purpose of God in order to continue clinging to the old rugged Cross and to remain connected to the Trinity. Little wonder the Scripture admonishes us to earnestly contend for the faith which was once delivered unto the saints – Jude 1:3. Beloved, once discipline is halted, destiny is truncated. Discipline informs your responsibility and spiritual sensitivity which establishes and sustains divine connectivity. More so, spiritual lethargy cannot manifest in the life of a disciplined man, because at every point in his life, he is watchful and prayerful. Discipline entails separating yourself from corrupters, separating yourself from polluters and pollutants, and blocking any element that undermines your relationship with God. If you condescend to the level of the world due to indiscipline, you will collapse with the world, and be condemned with it. Beware of indiscipline, because the junction of indiscipline is the break-point of our covenant intimate relationship with God. Discipline places you in grace but indiscipline displaces you from grace. In Romans 6:1-2, Apostle Paul asked, "Well then, should we keep on sinning so that God can show us more and more of His wonderful grace? Of course not! Since we have died to sin, how can we continue to live in it?" It is a Scriptural truth that indiscipline would ultimately divert you from God's agenda for your life and cause you to digress from the path of righteousness and glory. It is a fact that record-breakers, pace-setters, and trail-blazers are elevated on the wings of discipline. The essentiality of discipline is that it prevents you from relegating God to second place in your life. I've learned by experience and by the understanding of Scriptures that you'll be privy to divine information when you KISS the Son, but you need the discipline to process the information for your elevation. God speaks frequently to His children just as your earthly father would say at least a word to you or make a gesture to you whenever you are with him. I've heard God speak – softly and frankly, I've heard God sing, I've seen God write, I've seen God teach in His invisibility, I've heard God make a sound and seen Him make a gesture. But I didn't attain this sublime spiritual height without discipline. It took me vigils of prayers, vigils of praises, vigils of ruminating upon the word of God, seasons of fasting and sacrificial-giving, seasons of maintaining the integrity of faith and refusing to compromise, seasons of stewardship in the Church and seasons of evangelism in rough places and tough conditions. I still crave for more of God's fullness and grace, and more discipline until I see the Lord's face. Until I see the Lord face to face, I want to grow higher and go deeper in Him. However, discipline must be engaged consistently on my path if this would be established. Beloved, every good thing comes at a cost, and greatness in the Lord comes with a price, which is discipline. The disposition of Jesus Christ towards His sleeping disciples at the garden of Gethsemane authenticates the essentiality of discipline. In Matthew 26:40, He said, "couldn't you men keep watch with me for one hour?" In the preceding verses, Jesus Christ had instructed Peter and the other disciples to sit, while He set Himself apart to pray. But He returned to meet them sleeping. What an act of gross indiscipline! Note: Jesus didn't ask His disciples to pray along with Him in this context, He only asked them to **SIT** and He expected them to WATCH with Him. But they didn't sit, rather they slept. This account is basically telling us to SIT UP and WATCH continually until our Lord returns to take us Home. Sitting up in the Lord and watching on through prayers and supplication with thanksgiving connotes discipline. By the inference from Jesus' instruction to His disciples, endeavor to dedicate at least an hour of fervent worship to the Lord every day. Beloved, I urge you to be disciplined in engaging this daily commitment to worship for it provokes the ceaseless flow of marvelous grace and heavenly blessings. Note that investing in God's Kingdom through worship is the greatest investment that can ever be done. Therefore, be disciplined in worshipping the Lord with your entirety. As lovers, followers, and worshippers of Jesus Christ, we are called to dedicatedly SIT in His **S** – Service, in His **I** – Interests, and in His **T** – Truth. A man that is anxiously expecting the second coming of the Lord will not sit in the sit of the scornful. A heavenly-minded man will not tolerate any form of indiscipline, but a reprobate-minded man will. God is always communicating audibly or inaudibly to His children. He speaks continually to those who seek Him continually. A man who is always seeking to hear from God will never entertain indiscipline.

A man who craves divine attention and intervention would not allow indiscipline. A moment of indiscipline can greatly affect your spiritual sensitivity and divine connectivity. A man of discipline is a man who always rejects the devil's offers and always refuses to be defiled. He is a man who will always say "NO" when temptation comes knocking. A man of discipline is a man who will say "YES" to the Lord and "NO" to the world. No organization, spiritual or secular, can experience explosive and exponential growth without engaging discipline. A life void of discipline is a life void of purpose. Discipline is key to the success of an army. Engagement of discipline precedes the fulfillment of purpose. Dearly beloved, don't entertain indiscipline at any phase or stage of your life. Indiscipline depicts negligence, laxity, laziness, lukewarmness, nonchalance, a lack of fervency, and sinfulness. I beseech you to train and admonish your children, your entire household, your friends, and your congregation to imbibe the culture of discipline in the Lord. You just cannot downplay the essentiality of discipline in the fulfillment of destiny; for without discipline, destiny plunges into destruction. Assuredly, the destruction of destiny can be avoided by discipline. Discipline launches us into great heights of spirituality with God. Discipline enables us to go deep into the love of God. Engage discipline in kissing the Son. Put your body under subjection in order to remain a member of the covenantal body of Christ. Those who put their bodies under subjection for the sake of pleasing the Lord will shine forever as the stars of the firmament. I pray regularly in this manner due to my commitment to engaging discipline as I render my service to the Lord: Father, reprove me to improve and correct me to direct me. Those who want to remain firm in the Lord and do not want to go astray would pray in this manner. This prayer solidifies your discipline as you journey to destiny and it sanctifies you constantly as you render your service to the Lord, and as you prepare for the second coming of the Lord. Those who are reproved and corrected by God are those who are loved by Him and called according to His purpose. God loves you with great love and He wants you to stand firm for Him, even in the horrible perverseness of the world. Therefore, go all the way for the Lord with outright discipline in order to remain a member of the family of God. Live according to the teaching, standards, dictates, tenets, and principles of Christ. Discipline is essential to remaining fervent on the prayer altar which will ultimately prevent your destiny from being altered by the enemy. It takes discipline to fast and fasting fast-tracks you to your glorious destiny. Discipline is needed to keep your faith safeguarded! The demand for discipline compels us to adhere to, preach, and teach the Word of truth without adulterating it to suit personal philosophies. It takes discipline to give God quality high praise and to give sacrificially. A disciplined believer is a persistent worshipper of the Almighty Father, a relentless pursuer of the Heavenly vision, and a tenacious engager of the Word of Truth. A man given to discipline is willing to stretch himself in order to avoid becoming a wretch. It takes discipline to be sensitive to the move of the Holy Spirit. Discipline makes possible the lifestyle of simplicity, humility, and responsibility. It enables you to be proactive and it prevents you from being perverse.

Sometimes circumstances, nature, and environment may prompt you to compromise, but your resolve should always be, "come what may, I will KISS the Son." Hold on tenaciously to a lifestyle of discipline; for it takes discipline to KISS the Son. Do not let the enemy cut off your line of communication with God due to indiscipline. Indiscipline corrodes spirituality.

Beloved, do not be weary in keeping His Laws, in interacting with Him, in studying His Word, and in sacrificing for Him. KISS the Son, Ditch the sin! KISS the Son, Ditch the devil! Note: the Lord's anger blazes when you don't give Him kisses. So KISS the Son without reservation, and be sold out to Him and to His glorious gospel of the Kingdom of Heaven.

Here are some acronymical definitions of KISS in the context of this book with Scriptural backing:

KISS - Kingdom Initiative Self Sufficient. KISS - Kingdom Involvement Self Sustaining. KISS - Kingdom Insight Self Satisfying. KISS - Kingdom Intuition Self Sanctifying.

KISS the Son tirelessly. KISS the Son relentlessly. KISS the Son unflinchingly. KISS the Son unashamedly. KISS the Son eternally.

In all that you do, wherever you may be, in the Sun or the rain, in all conditions, against all odds, and come what may always remember to **KISS THE SON.**

PRAYER POINTS FOR INTIMACY WITH THE LORD

Here are some prayer points that will establish you in a flourishing and intimate covenant relationship with God:

1) Father, thank You for sending Your Son to reconcile me with You and to redeem me and restore me into the Abrahamic covenant relationship with You.

2) Father, terminate every power of darkness assigned to separate me from You in Jesus' mighty Name.

3) Lord, give me the grace to remain connected to You; let me never be disconnected from You in Jesus' Name.

4) Father, You are the Source of my life, let me never be cut off from You; be my Source of goodness, grace, glory, power, joy, and greatness forever in Jesus' Name.

5) Father, break every yoke of the devil planted to prevent me from serving you in the Name of Jesus.

6) Father, pull down every stronghold of wickedness assigned to pull me out of Your presence in Jesus' mighty Name.

7) Father, by the blood of Jesus, nullify every plan of the devil to break my relationship with you in Jesus' Name.

8) Father, by Your mercy, love, and grace, draw me close to You and uphold me in Your presence forever in Jesus' Name.

9) Father, uproot any unholy or sinful seed in me and plant the seed of righteousness in me in Jesus' Name.

10) Father, I surrender my totality to You and I desire to be intimate with You, grant my desire and use me for Your glory in Jesus' Name.

11) Father, please do not let Your presence depart from me and give me the grace to KISS you continually in Jesus' Name.

12) Father, I thank You for answering my prayers and granting my desires of having a flourishing and intimate covenant relationship with you.

SONG FOR KISS THE SON

The Holy Spirit inspired me with the song below in the process of writing this book. The link for this song can be found on the official social media pages of this book. Please go to the link to download the song, thereby knowing the tune.

SONG TITLE: KISS THE SON (Composed by Stephen A. Adeyemi, 2018)

CHORUS: I will KISS the Son, I will Love Him more, I will Honor Him - forevermore; I will KISS the Son, I will Love Him more, I will adore Him - forevermore

KISS the Son, KISS the Son, KISS the Son, Honor Him forevermore; KISS the Son, KISS the Son, adore Him forevermore.

VERSE 1: Omnipotent JESUS You reign, Lover of my soul, Ancient of Days; Oh my soul doth exalt your Name, You rule supreme, You rule sovereign. Ooooh

CHORUS: I will KISS the Son, I will Love Him more, I will Honor Him - forevermore; I will KISS the Son, I will Love Him more, I will adore Him – forevermore.

KISS the Son, KISS the Son, KISS the Son, Honor Him forevermore; KISS the Son, KISS the Son, adore Him forevermore.

VERSE 2: Whether in Sun or in the Rain, Oh I will KISS Him the God of all grace, for I know my Heavenly race, will end in Joy and the shout of praise. Ooooh

CHORUS: I will KISS the Son, I will Love Him more, I will Honor Him - forevermore; I will KISS the Son, I will Love Him more, I will adore Him - forevermore

KISS the Son, KISS the Son, KISS the Son, Honor Him forevermore; KISS the Son, KISS the Son, adore Him forevermore.

CHORUS: I will KISS the Son, I will Love Him more, I will Honor Him - forevermore; I will KISS the Son, I will Love Him more, I will adore Him – forever more

KISS the Son, KISS the Son, KISS the Son, Honor Him forevermore; KISS the Son, KISS the Son, adore Him forevermore.

CHORUS: I will KISS the Son, I will Love Him more, I will Honor Him - forevermore;

I will KISS the Son, I will Love Him more, I will adore Him - forevermore

KISS the Son, KISS the Son, KISS the Son, Honor Him forevermore; KISS the Son, KISS the Son, adore Him forevermore.

About the Author

Stephen Ayoola Adeyemi is a seasoned theologian, a member of the United Christian Ministerial Association and a minister of the Word. With a systematic, illustrative and expository approach to preaching the gospel of Christ, he dives passionately into the word of God by the leading of the Holy Spirit to bring about divine insights, deep revelations, and illumination to the message of the kingdom of God.

He is a dynamic and transformative speaker, who has lectured and impacted lives at various workshops, seminars, conferences, and churches in different parts of the world, and currently lectures at a Christian College. His life and ministry have transformed many to the glory of God.

Stephen is a Public Relations Consultant and a staunch advancer and advocate for transformational leadership. He holds a Bachelor's degree in Public Relations and Advertising and a Master's degree in Theology and Pastoral Leadership.

 @KissTheSonBook

 kissthesonbook@gmail.com

 @KisstheSonBook

 kissthesonbook

Made in the USA
Columbia, SC
23 July 2018